Cosmic kids 1
Workbook

Mia Kossiavelou

Pearson Education Limited
Edinburgh Gate
Harlow
Essex CM20 2JE
England
and Associated Companies throughout the world.

www.pearsonELT.com

© Pearson Education Limited 2012

The right of Mia Kossiavelou to be identified as author of this Work has been asserted by her in accordance with the Copyright, Designs and Patents Act 1988.

All rights reserved; no part of this publication may be reproduced, stored in a retrieval system, or transmitted in any form or by any means, electronic, mechanical, photocopying, recording, or otherwise without the prior written permission of the Publishers.

First published 2012
Fourteenth impression 2022

ISBN: 978-1-4082-4752-5

Set in Myriad Pro 11/17pt
Printed in Great Britain by Ashford Colour Press Ltd

Illustration Acknowledgements

Advocate Art (**Bryan Beach**) pages 6, 16, 24, 34, 42, 52, 59, 60, 70, 77, 78, 88); **Mike Moran** pages 4, 5, 6, 7, 11, 14, 16, 17, 22, 24, 26, 32, 34, 40, 41, 43, 45, 50, 51, 52, 55, 58, 62, 63, 68, 69, 70, 74, 78, 79, 80, 81, 86, 88, 94; **Illias Arahovitis** pages 5, 7, 8, 9, 11, 12, 14, 16, 18, 20, 21, 22, 25, 28, 30, 37, 38, 39, 42, 44, 48, 50, 51, 52, 53, 54, 57, 58, 60, 68, 71, 74, 78, 82, 84, 87, 90, 91, 92, 94.

Picture Credits

The publisher would like to thank the following for their kind permission to reproduce their photographs:

(Key: b-bottom; c-centre; l-left; r-right; t-top)

Alamy Images: Amana Images Inc. 48l, 83 (6), Bill Bachman 28c, Bailey-Cooper Photography 58, Mike Booth 46l, Christine Osborne Pictures 28b, discpicture 72 (Anaconda), Tim Hill 38t, Allan Ivy 82b, MIXA 10tl, Robert Harding Picture Library Ltd 56br, Tribaleye Images / J Marshall 20r, James Walker 51, 83 (3); **Art Directors and TRIP Photo Library:** Helene Rogers 38b; **Corbis:** Brand X 8, Image Source 66tc, 92 (2), image100 83 (1), Jose Luis Pelaez, Inc 36 (3), moodboard 82t, 86, Owen Franken 64, Jose Fuste Raga 66bl, 92 (3), Denis Scott 72 (Whale); **DK Images:** Andy Crawford 10br, Frank Greenaway 72 (Mosquito); **Fotolia.com:** Pavel Lysenko 12r; **Getty Images:** AFP / Toru Yamanaka 10tr, AFP / Toshifumi Kitamura 10bl, Nancy Brown 14, 20l, Grant Faint 12l, Hulton Archive / Dennis Hallinan 56tr, Taxi 83 (4); **Robert Harding World Imagery:** Michael Black 72 (Bull), Adam Woolfitt 66br, 92 (5); **iStockphoto:** Bernard Breton 72 (Penguins), Christoph Ermel 72 (Spider), Hans Van IJzendoorn 38tl, Mark Papas 13, Kristian Sekulic 36 (4), 47, 83 (2), soubrette 21, Stephanie Swartz 18; **Kobal Collection Ltd:** Universal / Wing Nut Films 74tr; **OnAsia Images:** Jesper Haynes 82tl; **Photolibrary.com:** Fotosearch 72 (Rabbit); **Press Association Images:** AP / Jerome Delay 28t, John Birdsall 46r; **Rex Features:** BEI / Matt Baron 70r, Paul Cooper 46c, c. Dreamworks / Everett 74tl, 83 (5), Per Lindgren 66tr, 92 (4), Robert Harding / Jack Jackson 20c, Alex Segre 56bl; **Shutterstock.com:** Orkhan Aslanov 56tl, Maksym Gorpenyuk 70l, Dmitriy Shironosov 36 (2); **Thinkstock:** Photodisc 66tl, 92 (1), Pixland 48r, Polka Dot Images 36 (1)

All other images © Pearson Education

Every effort has been made to trace the copyright holders and we apologise in advance for any unintentional omissions. We would be pleased to insert the appropriate acknowledgement in any subsequent edition of this publication.

Contents

Welcome to Cosmic Kids!	page 4
Unit 1	page 6
Unit 2	page 16
Unit 3	page 24
Unit 4	page 34
Unit 5	page 42
Unit 6	page 52
Unit 7	page 60
Unit 8	page 70
Unit 9	page 78
Unit 10	page 88

Welcome to Cosmic Kids!

1 Complete the alphabet.

A_a_ Bb Cc _d Ee F_ Gg
_h Ii J_ Kk _l M_ N_
Oo Pp _q Rr Ss _t U_
Vv _w _x Y_ Zz

2 Find and write the words and the numbers.

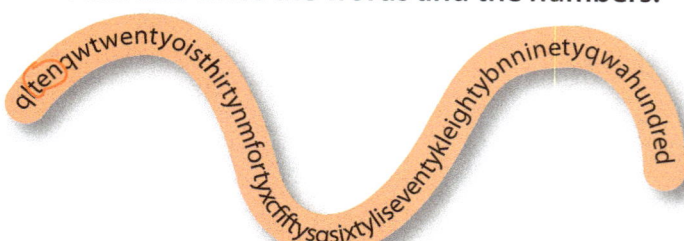

1 ten 10
2 _____
3 _____
4 _____
5 _____
6 _____
7 _____
8 _____
9 _____
10 _____

3 Write the colours.

1 uleprp   purple
2 kalbc   _____
3 dre   _____
4 leub   _____
5 twieh   _____
6 kipn   _____
7 rnwob   _____
8 renge   _____
9 wloeyl   _____
10 granoe   _____

4 Find the days of the week.

S U N D A Y Y T U
A D W F R I D A Y
T U E S D A Y P T
U Y D R T U D F H
R I N M O N D A U
D P E I R T B N R
A I S P L H G D S
Y W D W U H A N D
U I A T H U R S A
P U Y M O N D A Y

5 Complete the months.

1 J_a_n_u_ar_y_
2 _e_ru___y
3 ___r_h
4 A___i_
5 M___
6 ___n_
7 J_l_
8 A___u_t
9 _e_te_ber
10 O_t_be_
11 No___m___r
12 _e___mber

6 Write the words and circle *a* or *an*.

1 a /(an) ice cream

2 a / an b_____

3 a / an u_____

4 a / an e_____

5 a / an o_____

6 a / an d_____

7 a / an c_____

8 a / an a_____

9 a / an g_____

7 Complete the numbers and the plurals.

1 s _i_ _x_ mi_ _c_ _e_

2 t _ _ _ _ _   b _ _ _ _ _ _

3 t _ _ _   f _ _ _ _

4 f _ _ _ _   t _ _ _ _ _ _ _

5 s _ _ _ _ _   t _ _ _ _ _

6 f _ _ _ _   c _ _ _ _ _ _ _ _ _

7 e _ _ _ _ _   b _ _ _ _ _

8 Circle the correct words.
1 'Is / (Are) Ellie and Alex friends?' 'Yes, they (are) / is.'
2 We *are* / *am* students.
3 'Are / Is he Greek?' 'Yes, he *is* / *are*.'
4 You *aren't* / *is not* English.
5 'Are *I* / *you* a teacher?' 'Yes, I *am* / *are*.'
6 They *aren't* / He *isn't* brothers.
7 The cat *is* / *am* black.

9 Write questions and short answers.
1 you / English (✘)
Are you English?
No, I'm not.

2 we / friends (✔)
_ _ _ _ _ _ _ _ _ _ _ _ _ _ _ _ _ _ _ ?
_ _ _ _ _ _ _ _ _ _ _ _ _ _ _ _ _ _ _ .

3 she / a teacher (✔)
_ _ _ _ _ _ _ _ _ _ _ _ _ _ _ _ _ _ _ ?
_ _ _ _ _ _ _ _ _ _ _ _ _ _ _ _ _ _ _ .

4 they / sisters? (✘)
_ _ _ _ _ _ _ _ _ _ _ _ _ _ _ _ _ _ _ ?
_ _ _ _ _ _ _ _ _ _ _ _ _ _ _ _ _ _ _ .

5 it / September (✔)
_ _ _ _ _ _ _ _ _ _ _ _ _ _ _ _ _ _ _ ?
_ _ _ _ _ _ _ _ _ _ _ _ _ _ _ _ _ _ _ .

10 Complete the words with *a, e, i, o* and *u*.

1 d _o_ _o_ r
2 b _ _ r d
3 ch _ _ r
4 t _ _ ch _ r
5 p _ n
6 p _ nc _ l
7 r _ bb _ r
8 c _ mp _ t _ r
9 d _ sk
10 b _ _ k

11 Write the times.

1  *It's half past three.*

2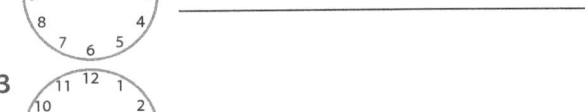

3

4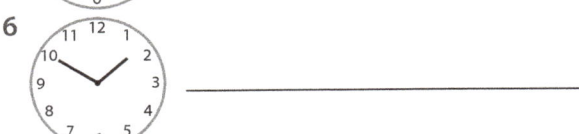

5

6

12 Write your name.

Hi, my name's _ .

1a Ellie and Alex

Vocabulary

1 Match the pictures to the sentences.

A Who are those people?

B What's that green thing? Is it a hat?

C That's our cat.

D This is my bike.

E I'm Ellie. And this is my parrot, Echo.

2 Write the words.

1 oimlbe hnpoe — *mobile phone*
2 mesarun _____
3 SGP _____
4 oblisuanrc _____
5 prorerte _____
6 igaldit arcema _____

3 Look at the family tree and write the words.

brother   father   grandfather   ~~grandmother~~
mother   sister

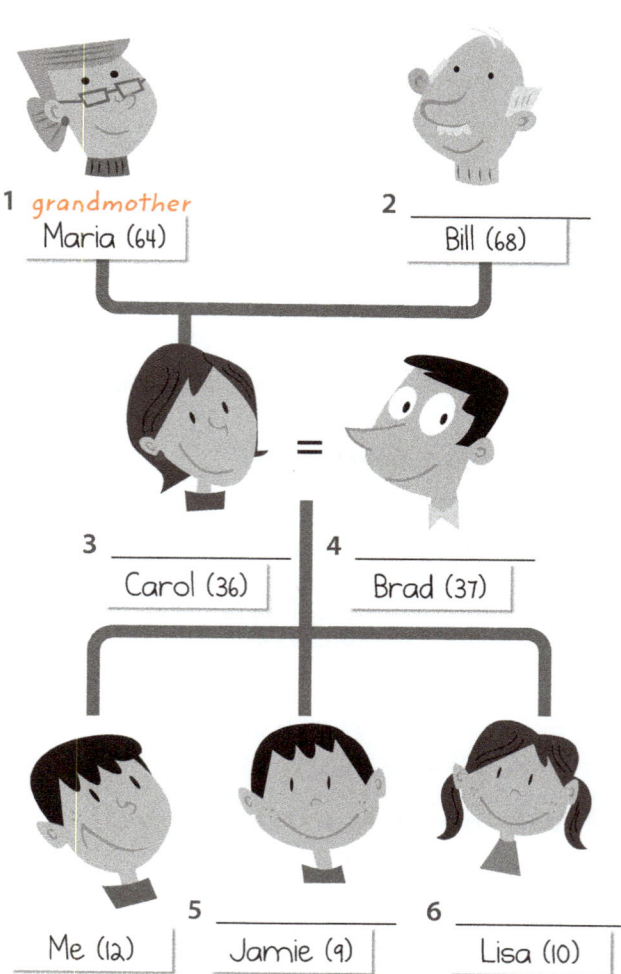

1 *grandmother* Maria (64)
2 _____ Bill (68)
3 _____ Carol (36)
4 _____ Brad (37)
5 _____ Me (12) / Jamie (9)
6 _____ Lisa (10)

4 Read the sentences and write *True* (T) or *False* (F).

1 My mother's sister is my cousin. [F]
2 My father's father is my grandfather. [ ]
3 My grandfather's son is my aunt. [ ]
4 My dad's mother is my grandmother. [ ]
5 My mother's sister is my brother. [ ]
6 My father's brother is my uncle. [ ]
7 My grandmother's daughter is my mother. [ ]

Grammar

5 Circle the correct words.
1. (This) / These is my grandmother.
2. That / Those are my cousins.
3. This / These is a parrot.
4. This / These are our bikes.
5. That / Those is a digital camera.
6. This / These are our mobile phones.
7. That / Those are their notebooks.
8. That / These is his box.
9. These / This is my dad.
10. Those / That are her cats.

6 Write the sentences in the plural form.
1. This is a cat. — These are cats.
2. That is a mouse. _____
3. This is an egg. _____
4. This is a foot. _____
5. That is a pencil. _____
6. This is a bike. _____
7. That is a baby. _____
8. That is a rubber. _____
9. This is a door. _____
10. That is an ice cream. _____

7 Write sentences. Use *this*, *that*, *these* and *those* and the words below.

> bike binoculars cars children digital camera
> fish mobile phone reporter

These are binoculars.

_____

_____

_____

_____

_____

_____   _____

1b Your world

Vocabulary

1 Complete the email with words from the box.

> ~~sunglasses~~ tent money pocket
> surfboard pet

Hi,

My name is Jack. I've got lots of things. These are my ¹ sunglasses. They're amazing! My favourite thing is my ² _____. I've got a ³ _____. I've got some ⁴ _____ in my ⁵ _____. I've got a ⁶ _____ dog. Her name is Dido. Here is my photo.

2 Circle the odd one out.

1 goldfish   kitten   (glasses)
2 computer game   keys   mp3 player
3 hamster   comic   book
4 bird   bike   car

3 Complete the sentences with words from the box.

> bird glasses money ~~hamster~~ pocket pet

1 My hamster is small and brown.
2 I've got _____ in my bag. Look, €10.
3 We have got a new _____. It's a white kitten.
4 My _____ are on my head.
5 That _____ is pink and grey. It's a parrot.
6 'What's in your _____?' 'My keys and my mobile phone.'

4 Find the animal words and write them.

B	I	R	D	K	G	P	A
A	C	I	R	I	V	A	F
H	A	M	S	T	E	R	M
S	T	Y	X	T	C	R	I
D	B	E	I	E	L	O	T
O	P	S	C	N	J	T	A
G	O	L	D	F	I	S	H

1 bird
2 _____
3 _____
4 _____
5 _____
6 _____
7 _____

Grammar

5 Match.

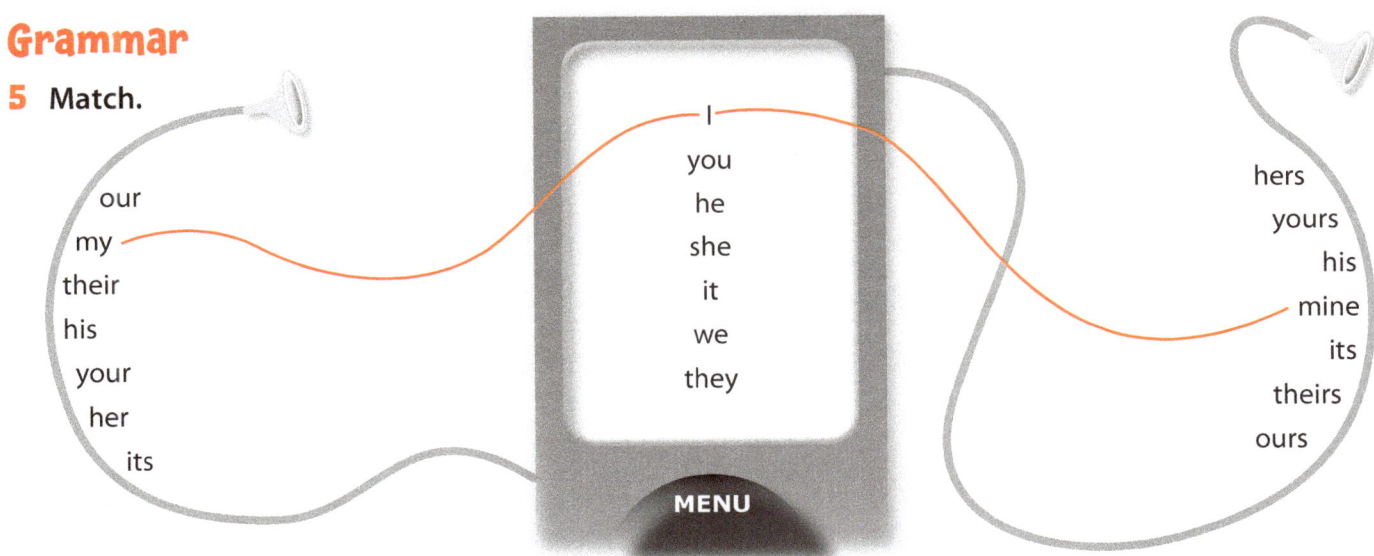

our —
my — mine
their
his
your
her
its

I
you
he
she
it
we
they

hers
yours
his
mine
its
theirs
ours

6 Circle the correct words.
1 I / **My** mobile phone is great!
2 He / His has got an amazing surfboard.
3 Are these keys your / yours?
4 Look at that dog. What's its / it's name?
5 This tent is theirs / their.
6 These are we / our cousins.
7 What's her / she surname?

7 Look at the pictures and complete the sentences. Use possessive adjectives or possessive pronouns.

1. That is *her* favourite photo.
4. That comic is _____.
2. These are _____ sweets.
5. This is a goldfish. _____ name is Goldie.
3. Is this _____ money? Yes, thank you. It's _____.
6. Those are _____ bikes.

8 Read the sentences and circle the correct words.
1 I **have** / has got a kitten, but I hasn't / **haven't** got a goldfish.
2 You have / has got an mp3 player, but you hasn't / haven't got a mobile phone.
3 He hasn't / haven't got a digital camera, but he has / have got a surfboard.
4 She has / have got a brother, but she hasn't / haven't got a sister.
5 We have / has got a hamster, but we haven't / hasn't got a goldfish.
6 They haven't / hasn't got money, but they have / has got friends.
7 The parrot haven't / hasn't got a name, but it has / have got beautiful colours.

9 Complete the sentences with have/has got (✔) or haven't/hasn't got (✘).
1 You *have got* cool sunglasses. (✔)
2 Alice _____ a pet hamster. (✘)
3 Patch the dog _____ white and brown feet. (✔)
4 Jack _____ a red surfboard. (✘)
5 We _____ amazing things! (✔)
6 Luke, Alice and Jake _____ great photos. (✔)
7 His cousins _____ mp3 players. (✘)
8 I _____ keys in my bag. (✘)

1c Cosmic world

Vocabulary

1 Label the pictures with words from the box.

> books   hamsters   kimono   school uniform
> temple

1 school uniform
2 _____
3 _____
4 _____
5 _____

2 Find the words. Then complete the sentences.

ficapitalewnfestivalruqletteraznprizeouytemplebvuniformpc

1 The *capital* of Japan is Tokyo.
2 I've got a _____ from my friend in Greece.
3 There's a music _____ this weekend. Let's go.
4 Look at that Japanese _____. It's beautiful.
5 'What's the first _____?' 'It's a digital camera.'
6 They've got a blue and white _____ at their school.

3 Complete the crossword puzzle.

1 across: H A M S T E R
2 across: K _ _ _ _
3 across: C _ _ _ _ _
4 down: F
5 down: _

ACROSS

1 I've got a pet. It's a brown and white *hamster*.
2 That Japanese woman has got a _____.
3 All countries have got _____ cities.

DOWN

4 Jan has got a _____ for her letter.
5 This pop _____ is great fun!

4 Look at the table. Then read the sentences and write *True* (T) or *False* (F).

Name	Poppy
Age	10
Nationality	English
Pet	hamster
Pet's name	Fluffy
Colour of pet	brown and white
Favourite things	mp3 player, glasses, phone

1 Her name is Poppy. T
2 She's eleven years old. ☐
3 She's from England. ☐
4 She's got a kitten. ☐
5 Her pet hasn't got a name. ☐
6 Her hamster's brown and white. ☐
7 She has got four favourite things. ☐

10

Grammar

5 Match the questions and short answers.

1. Have you got an mp3 player, Riku?
2. Have they got a Greek surname?
3. Has the bird got a name?
4. Has John got a notebook?
5. Has Liza got a prize?
6. Have you and Dan got school uniforms at your school?

A No, we haven't.
B Yes, he has.
C No, I haven't.
D Yes, they have.
E Yes, it has.
F No, she hasn't.

6 Complete the questions with *have* or *has*.

1. *Have* you got a pet dog?
2. _____ Greece got temples?
3. _____ they got surfboards?
4. _____ your dad got a bike?
5. _____ your teacher got a computer?
6. _____ we got kimonos?
7. _____ your brother got sweets?

7 Write questions with *have* or *has got*. Then answer for you.

1. you / mp3 player
   Have you got an MP3 player?
   Yes, I have./No, I haven't.
2. your mum / a mobile phone
   _____?
   _____.
3. your best friend / a digital camera
   _____?
   _____.
4. your country / temples
   _____?
   _____.
5. you and your friend / letters
   _____?
   _____.
6. students in your country / school uniforms
   _____?
   _____.

8 Complete the table for you. Then write sentences with *have* or *has got*.

	Pet	Mobile phone	Prize
Sally	✔	✔	✘
Harry	✘	✘	✔
Simon & Julie	✘	✔	✘
You			

1. Has Sally got a pet and a mobile phone.
   Yes, she has.
2. Has Harry got a prize?
   _____.
3. Have Simon and Julie got a pet?
   _____.
4. Have you got a mobile phone?
   _____.
5. Has Sally got a prize?
   _____.
6. Have you got a pet?
   _____.

9 Correct the punctuation.

H
~~h~~i,
M
~~m~~y name's danny. i live in London. it's the capital of England. my birthday is on saturday the 18th of september. this is a photo of my pet parrot, prince. he's green and red. he's amazing! have you got a pet? are you english too?
bye,
danny

11

Reading

1 Read the text. Then write the words.

1 Patrick is *thirteen* years old.

2 This is his _____.

13

Friends Club

My name's Patrick. I'm Irish and I'm from Dublin. I'm thirteen years old. I've got a computer. It's great! It's got amazing games. It's my favourite thing. What's your favourite thing?

I've got a new mobile phone. It's black. It's fantastic. Look at this photo of my sister. Her name's Jane. She's six years old.

I've got lots of friends. My best friend's name is Simon. He's thirteen too and he's in my class at school. Have you got a best friend? Simon's got two pet hamsters. They're called Fluffy and Benji. They're brown and white. Have you got a pet?

3 He has got a _____.

4 These are Simon's _____.

2 Read the text again and circle the correct answers.

1 What is Patrick's favourite thing?
   a his game
   b his computer

2 What colour is Patrick's mobile phone?
   a black
   b brown and white

3 Simon is Patrick's
   a pet.
   b best friend.

4 Fluffy and Benji are
   a hamsters.
   b brother and sister.

3 Read Laura's email and complete her member profile.

Hi Patrick,

I'm Laura and I'm thirteen. I'm from Rome, Italy. I've got a computer, but it isn't my favourite thing. My favourite thing is my mp3 player. It's purple and white.

Your mobile phone is great and your sister is very pretty. I've got one brother and one sister. My brother Paolo is ten and he is crazy! My sister Claudia is fifteen. Claudia is always with her friends, but I've got my friends too.

I've got a pet dog. His name is Sparky and he's grey and white. He's a great dog. He's my best friend. He's ten years old. Have you got a dog?

Write soon,

Laura

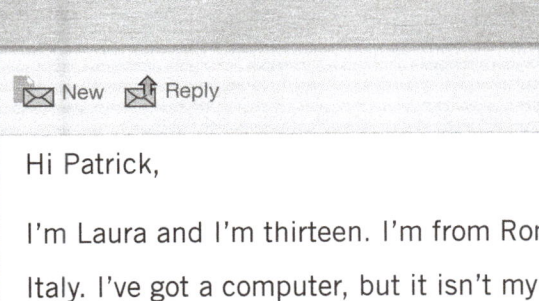

Friends' Club

Member Profile

Name:
....

Age:
....

City & country:
....

Brothers/sisters: ....
Favourite thing: ....
Pets: ....

Writing

4 Write an email to Laura. Follow this plan.
Hi Laura,
Paragraph 1:
your name, age, city/town and country, favourite thing
Paragraph 2:
your family and friends
Paragraph 3:
your pets
Write soon,
(your name)

Review 1

Vocabulary

1 Circle the correct words.

1 (GPS) / mp3 player

4 binoculars / sunglasses

2 keys / money

5 temple / tent

3 pocket / kimono

6 pet / reporter

2 Complete the family words.

1 b r o t h er
2 s _ _ t _ r
3 g _ a _ d _ ot _ _ r
4 d _ _ g _ ter
5 a _ _ _ _
6 un _ _ _ _
7 c _ _ _ s _ _
8 mo _ h _ _ _
9 f _ _ h _ _ _
10 s _ _ _

3 Complete the crossword puzzle.

Across/Down clues with letters shown:
- 1 Down: M O B I L E P H O N E
- 2 Down: G
- 3 Across: B _ _ _
- 4 Down: S
- 5 Across: D _ _ _ _ _ _ L C _ _ _
- 6 Across: K _ _ E

1

4

2

5

3

6

Grammar

4 Choose the correct answers.

1 _____ is my sister Jane and that's my brother Jim.
  a (This)   b These

2 These are my glasses and _____ are my keys.
  a that   b those

3 _____ book is his.
  a That   b Those

4 _____ binoculars are black.
  a This   b These

5 _____ apple is red.
  a This   b Those

5 Circle the correct words.
1 That's not my bag. *Mine* / *My* is blue.
2 This is Fiona and *her* / *hers* brother.
3 Look! This is *ours* / *our* new parrot Pirate.
4 My mobile phone is red, but *your* / *yours* is black.
5 *Their* / *Theirs* school uniforms are blue and white.
6 This prize is *he* / *his*.

6 Complete the sentences with *have got*, *haven't got*, *has got* or *hasn't got*.
1 I *have got* a new computer game. (✓)
2 Mike _____ brown eyes. (✗)
3 We _____ a new teacher. (✓)
4 Tom _____ a dog. (✗)
5 Anna _____ pink binoculars. (✓)
6 Jill and Jane _____ school uniforms. (✗)

7 Write questions and short answers.
1 a dog / have / you / got
   Have you got a dog?
   Yes, I have.
2 have / got / Maria and Poppy / brown eyes
   _____?
   Yes, _____.
3 Peter / a surfboard / got / has
   _____?
   No, _____.
4 we / got / have / a new teacher
   _____?
   Yes, _____.
5 a computer game / you / got / have
   _____?
   Yes, _____.
6 Sue / got / keys / has
   _____?
   No, _____.

8 Complete the blog.

My Cosmic Blog!

What is your name?
_____
_____

How old are you?
_____
_____

Have you got a brother or a sister?
_____
_____
_____

Have you got a pet?
_____
_____

Colour the Stars

0-8 mistakes:
Brilliant work!

9-15 mistakes:
Great work!

More than 15 mistakes:
Good try. Revise and try again!

2a Where is Bianca?

Vocabulary

1 Look at the pictures and write *True* (T) or *False* (F).

 Alex meets Mrs Pappas.

 Gran hasn't got a problem. ☐

 This is Bianca's favourite chair. ☐

 Bianca is in her favourite tree. ☐

 These are pills. ☐

2 Complete the crossword puzzle.

1 P I L L S
3 C
4 V
5 G
6 T

3 Label the picture with these words.

> balcony   bathroom   bedroom   floor   garden
> kitchen   living room   ~~pool~~   toilet   window

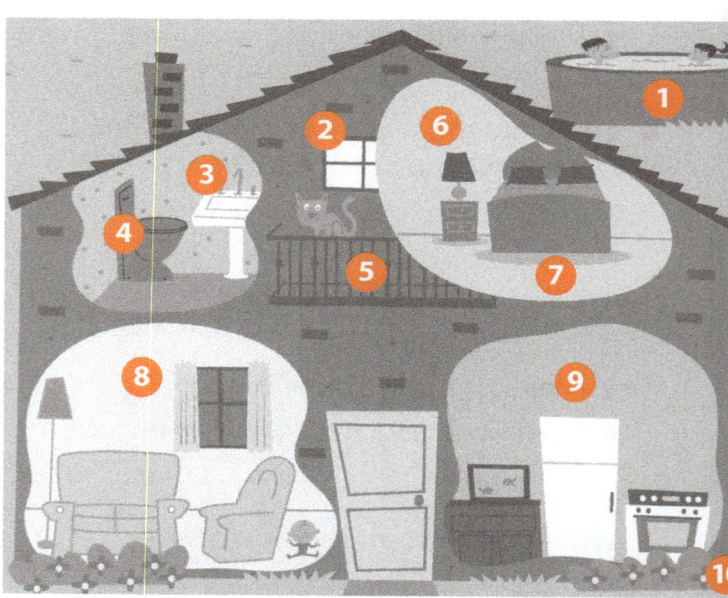

1 pool
2 _____
3 _____
4 _____
5 _____
6 _____
7 _____
8 _____
9 _____
10 _____

4 Complete the sentences about the house in Exercise 3. Use *behind*, *in*, *next to*, *on* and *under*.

1 The kitten is *on* the balcony.
2 The baby is _____ the chair.
3 The children are _____ the pool.
4 The window is _____ the bedroom.
5 The living room is _____ the bathroom.

Grammar

5 Circle the correct answers.

1 _____ a camera on the table.
  a (There is)
  b There are

2 _____ four children in the house.
  a There is
  b There are

3 _____ any CDs in my bedroom.
  a There isn't
  b There aren't

4 _____ flowers on the balcony?
  a Is there
  b Are there

5 _____ a pool in the garden.
  a There isn't
  b Isn't there

6 _____ a toilet in the bathroom.
  a There is
  b There are

7 _____ a table on the grass?
  a Is there
  b Are there

6 Complete the sentences with *There is* and *There are*.

1 *There is* a window in my bedroom.
2 _____ six chairs in the kitchen.
3 _____ a mobile phone on the table.
4 _____ three CDs next to the television.
5 _____ three birds on the balcony.
6 _____ a strange comic on the chair.

7 Look at Exercise 6 and write negative sentences. Use *There isn't* and *There aren't*.

1 *There isn't a window in my bedroom.*
2 _____
3 _____
4 _____
5 _____
6 _____

8 Look at the picture and circle the correct words.

1 Is there a ball under the table?
  (Yes, there is.) / No, there isn't.
2 Are there two mice behind the bag?
  Yes, *there are.* / *there is.*
3 Is there a glove on the table?
  No, there *isn't* / *aren't*.
4 Is there a digital camera in the bag?
  Yes, there is. / No, there isn't.
5 Is there a kitten in the bag?
  Yes, there *is* / *are*.
6 Is there a notebook beside the ball?
  Yes, there is. / No, there isn't.

9 Complete the questions with *Is there* and *Are there*. Then answer for you.

1 *Is there* a television in your bedroom?
  Yes, there is./No, there isn't.
2 _____ a table in your kitchen?
  _____
3 _____ a surfboard in your bedroom?
  _____
4 _____ plants in your house?
  _____
5 _____ pets in your house?
  _____

17

2b Your world

Vocabulary

1 Circle the correct words.

1. cage / computer

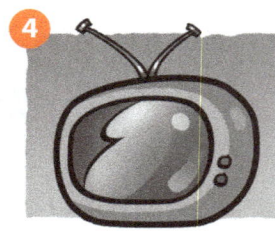
4. poster / television

2. CDs / teddy bear

5. television / CDs

3. poster / cage

6. computer / teddy bear

2 Match the pictures to the words.

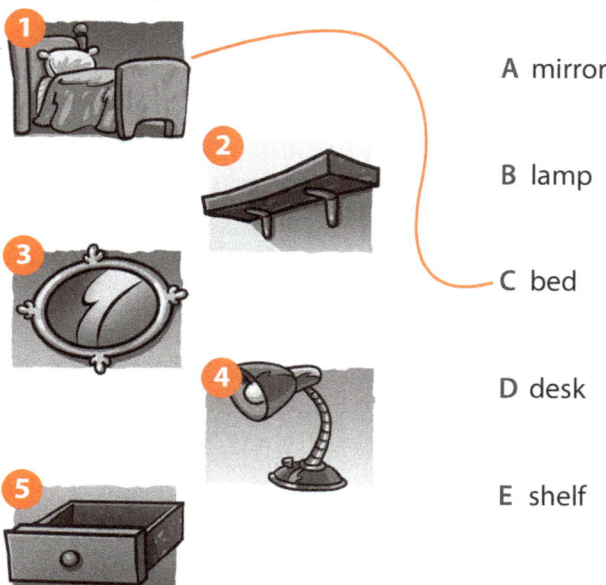

A mirror
B lamp
C bed
D desk
E shelf
F drawer

3 Complete the words and write *Yes* or *No* about your house.

1 There's a *lamp* (mpal) in our living room. *Yes*
2 There's one _____ (edb) in my bedroom. ____
3 There's a _____ (rmoirr) in the bathroom. ____
4 There is a _____ (fselh) with CDs in my bedroom. ____
5 Dad has got a _____ (sdke) in the garage. ____
6 There's a _____ (wrdear) next to my bed. ____

4 Find and write the words.

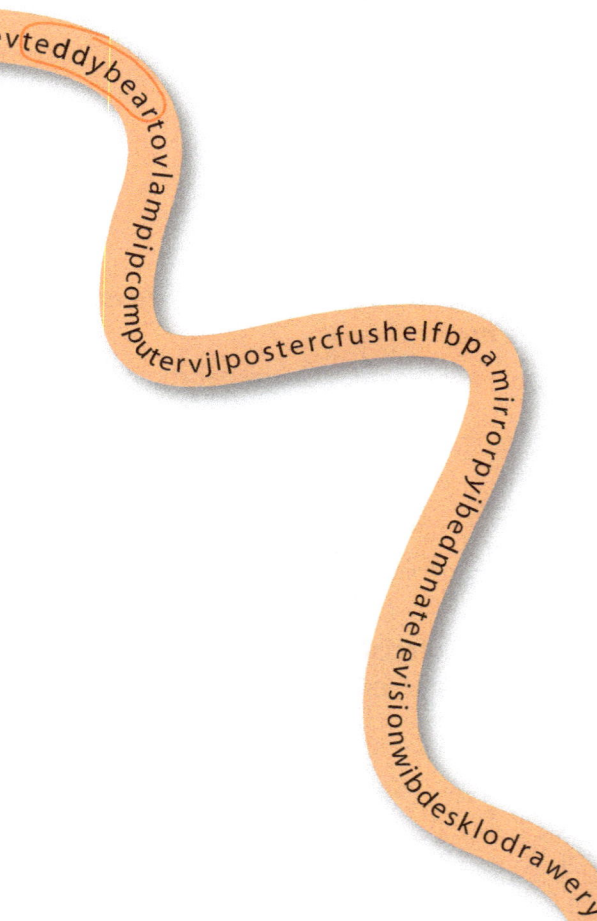

1 teddy bear
2 _____
3 _____
4 _____
5 _____
6 _____
7 _____
8 _____
9 _____
10 _____

Grammar

5 Put a tick (✔) or a cross (✘). Correct the wrong sentences.
1. Is that John's computer? ✔
2. Helens' birthday is on Friday. *Helen's*
3. Rob's best friend is Jason. _____
4. The cats' name is Blackie. _____
5. My parents' car is blue. _____
6. My sister's bedrooms are beautiful. _____
7. The womens' toilet is beside the kitchen. _____
8. The children's toys are on the floor. _____

6 Choose the correct answers.
1. Where are _____ keys?
   - **a Anna's**
   - b Annas'
2. _____ pool is great!
   - a Justin's
   - b Justins'
3. My pet _____ name is Robby.
   - a dogs'
   - b dog's
4. These are the _____ teddy bears.
   - a children's
   - b childrens'
5. That _____ car is amazing.
   - a reporter's
   - b reporters'
6. Our _____ house is in London.
   - a grandparent's
   - b grandparents'
7. My _____ names are Helen and Michael.
   - a cousins'
   - b cousin's
8. Those _____ are ours!
   - a digital cameras'
   - b digital cameras

7 Read and put apostrophes.

> Hi everyone,
> This is my house. It has got a living room, a kitchen, a bathroom and three bedrooms. My brother's bedroom is very big. His name is Jason. He has got a bed, a desk and a television in his room. Jasons bed is under the window. He has also got a pet parrot. The parrots cage is white. My parents room is next to Jasons. It's small and it has only got a bed. My room is next to my parents room. It's also my sisters room. Her name is Petra. Petras bed is under my bed. We've got bunk beds! There are two pets in our room – a kitten and a hamster. Our pets toys are on the floor. Have you got any pets?

8 Complete the sentences. Use the words in the brackets with an apostrophe *'s* or *s'*.
1. What colour is your *parents'* bedroom? (parents)
2. Where are your _____ CDs? (mum)
3. What are your _____ names? (two best friends)
4. Where is your favourite _____ house? (aunt)
5. What are your _____ surnames? (grandparents)

9 Answer the questions in Exercise 7 about you. Use apostrophe *'s* or *s'*.
1. _____.
2. _____.
3. _____.
4. _____.
5. _____.

2c Cosmic world

Vocabulary

1 Look at the questions. Choose the correct answers about homes around the world.

Homes around the world			
1 Where is this home?	a Mongolia (circled) b England	a Japan b Yemen	a England b Greece
2 What is it?	a a house b a big tent	a flats b yurts	a a houseboat b a flat
3 What has it got?	a a balcony b one room	a white windows b a garden	a brown walls b a fantastic view

2 Match the words to the pictures.

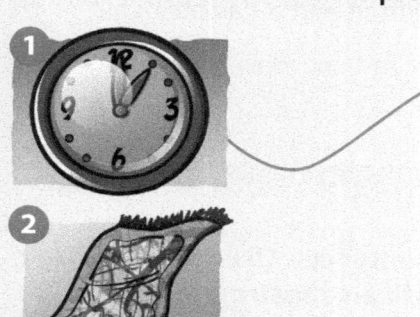

A carpet
B clock
C cupboard
D flat
E shower
F view

(1 matched to B clock)

3 Find and write the house words.

V	P	L	A	N	T	S	F	S
I	N	R	T	H	O	C	V	F
E	K	K	J	O	I	M	L	L
W	T	N	A	M	P	V	E	A
H	O	U	S	E	B	O	A	T

1 plants
2 _____
3 _____
4 _____
5 _____

4 Complete the sentences.

1 There's a c u p b o a r d for my things. (puobcard)
2 There's a _____ on the houseboat. (hoswre)
3 The _____ is fantastic. (wevi)
4 There's a nice brown and yellow _____ on the floor. (tecapr)
5 'What time is it?' 'Look at the _____ on the wall.' (lcokc)
6 They've got some plants in the _____. (laft)

20

Grammar

5 Circle the correct answers.

1 _____ in the flat next to you?
   a (Who's)   b Whose
2 _____ is this schoolbag?
   a Who's   b Whose
3 _____ your best friend?
   a Whose   b Who's
4 _____ amazing car is that?
   a Whose   b Who's
5 _____ fantastic posters are these?
   a Who's   b Whose
6 _____ on the houseboat?
   a Whose   b Who's

6 Complete the dialogues with *Whose* or *Who's*.

1 *Whose* is this bedroom? — It's Jane's.
2 _____ are those computer games? — They're my brother's.
3 _____ at home? — My parents and my sister.
4 _____ in that poster? — It's Beyoncé.
5 _____ his friend? — Steve is his friend.
6 _____ are those teddy bears? — They're the children's.
7 _____ is the cage? — It's my hamster's.

7 Circle the correct word.

1 There are six people (but) / or there is only one room in the large tent.
2 There are two posters, a mirror *and* / *but* two shelves on my wall.
3 Is your home a flat *but* / *or* is it a house?
4 He has got a cat *or* / *but* he hasn't got a dog.
5 I've got a digital camera *and* / *but* a mobile phone.
6 My flat has got a nice balcony *but* / *or* it hasn't got a good view.

8 Complete the description with *and*, *but* and *or*.

My home is a flat in Athens. There are three bedrooms, a living room ¹ *and* a kitchen. My bedroom is purple ² _____ green. It's nice, ³ _____ it's small. There are posters ⁴ _____ shelves on the walls. We haven't got a garden, ⁵ _____ we've got a balcony. I play in my bedroom ⁶ _____ on the balcony after school. There isn't a view of the sea ⁷ _____ the mountains from the balcony, ⁸ _____ it's got a lot of plants.

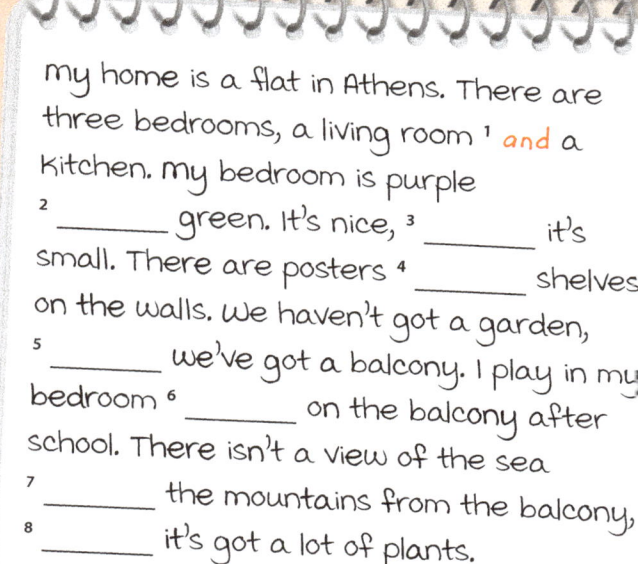

Vocabulary

1 Look at the picture and circle the correct words.

1 The computer is *next to* / *on* the teddy bear.
2 The desk is *on* / *in* the bedroom.
3 The door is *in* / *under* the clock.
4 The cat poster is *on* / *behind* the bed.
5 The mirror is *in* / *on* the wall.

2 Complete the table.

balcony bathroom bed carpet clock
desk garden kitchen lamp living room
mirror toilet

Room / Place	Furniture / Thing
1 balcony	6 _____
2 _____	7 _____
3 _____	8 _____
4 _____	9 _____
5 _____	10 _____
	11 _____
	12 _____

3 Look and complete.

What is it?

1 It's a *clock*.

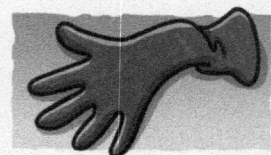

2 It's a _____.

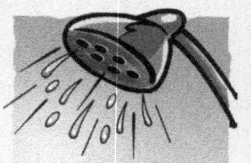

3 It's a _____.

4 It's a _____.

5 It's a _____.

6 It's a _____.

7 It's a _____.

Grammar

4 Circle the correct possessive.
1 (Beyoncé's) / Beyoncés' songs are great!
2 Where are the women's / womens' toilets?
3 My friends' / friend's name is Barnaby Crump.
4 What colour is your parent's / parents' room?
5 This is the childrens' / children's classroom.
6 Dads' / Dad's book is on the table.

5 Complete the sentences with There is, There are, Is there or Are there.
1 *Is there* a television in the bedroom?
2 _____ posters on your wall?
3 _____ a strange dog next to the pool. Whose is it?
4 _____ sweets in the cupboard.
5 _____ a surfboard on the balcony.
6 _____ a kitten in the garden?
7 _____ books on my bed.
8 _____ CDs on that shelf?

6 Complete the questions with Whose or Who's.
1 *Whose* keys are these?
2 _____ your best friend?
3 _____ computer is this?
4 _____ in the classroom?
5 _____ brother has got a car?
6 _____ in the bathroom?
7 _____ desk is this?
8 _____ in bed?
9 _____ bicycle is that?

7 Complete the blog.

My Cosmic Blog!

Me and my home

My name is _____ . I'm from _____ . There are _____ in my family. Our home is _____ . It has got _____ . My bedroom is _____ . There is _____ and _____ in my room, but there isn't _____ .

Colour the stars

0-8 mistakes:
Brilliant work!

9-15 mistakes:
Great work!

More than 15 mistakes:
Good try. Revise and try again!

3a A famous cat!

Vocabulary

1 Look at the pictures and write *True* (T) or *False* (F).

1. There are two gloves and pills under the tree. [F]

2. Echo is missing. [ ]

3. Bianca is famous and has got prizes. [ ]

4. Bianca never sits in that chair. [ ]

5. Gran has got Bianca's toys. [ ]

6. Vinny finds Bianca. [ ]

2 Complete the sentences with these words.

> breakfast ~~expensive~~ famous sit
> missing Don't worry

1. This digital camera is very *expensive*. Be careful!
2. Beyoncé, Madonna and Justin Timberlake are _____ singers.
3. Bianca's not here. She's _____ .
4. _____ ! No problem!
5. That's my chair. I _____ there.
6. I have _____ at half past seven in the morning.

3 Match the sentences to the pictures.

1. Jim does puzzles. [C]
2. Tom takes photos with his new digital camera. [ ]
3. Pia plays the piano. [ ]
4. Max rides a bike. [ ]
5. Pam collects stamps. [ ]
6. Kate goes out with friends. [ ]

4 Complete the sentences with these words.

> collect do go ride play ~~take~~

1. You *take* nice photos.
2. I _____ my bike to school.
3. They _____ stamps from around the world.
4. I _____ chess with Dad.
5. We _____ out with friends in the afternoon.
6. I _____ puzzles with my brother.

Grammar

5 Choose the correct answers.

1 We _____ our new computer.
  a (love) b loves
2 My grandmother _____ famous people on television.
  a watches b watch
3 John _____ Japanese and French.
  a study b studies
4 You _____ out with friends on Fridays.
  a goes b go
5 Your camera _____ brilliant photos.
  a take b takes
6 Those dogs _____ all day.
  a plays b play
7 I _____ to music in my bedroom.
  a listen b listens
8 Dad _____ breakfast at eight o'clock.
  a have b has

6 Look at the table. Then read the sentences and write Yes or No.

	Andrew	Irene
Ride a bike	✔	✔
Watch animal programmes on televison	✗	✔
Play computer games	✔	✔
Collect stamps	✗	✔
Listen to music	✔	✔
Go out with friends	✔	✔
Take photos	✔	✗
Do puzzles	✗	✔

1 Andrew and Irene ride bikes. Yes
2 Andrew watches animal programmes on television. ____
3 They play computer games. ____
4 Irene collects stamps. ____
5 They listen to music and go out with friends. ____
6 Andrew does puzzles. ____
7 Irene takes photos. ____

7 Complete the sentences. Use the correct form of these words.

have   listen   play   study   wash   watch

I *study* every day after dinner.

My brother _____ DVDs on his computer.

Our dog _____ football!

Charlie _____ breakfast every morning.

Carmen _____ to music on her mp3 player.

8 Read and complete.

Harry and Helen ¹ *have* (have) breakfast at half past seven. At quarter to eight Helen ² _____ (go) to school with her mum. Helen ³ _____ (carry) her books in her backpack. She ⁴ _____ (sit) next to me and she's a very good student. She ⁵ _____ (like) school and she ⁶ _____ (study) every day. Harry is her brother. He's three years old and he ⁷ _____ (stay) at home with his granny. She ⁸ _____ (read) his favourite books about animals.

3b Your world

Vocabulary

1 Complete the crossword puzzle.

```
    1
    M
    A
    G
 2  A
 P  _  _  _
    Z      3
    I      F
 4  N   5
 D  _  _   J _ _
    E
 6
 L  _  _  _  _
```

ACROSS
2 You use colours to _____ .
4 We always _____ orange juice in the morning.
5 My mum's a teacher. What's your mum's _____?
6 Do you drink _____?

DOWN
1 I read a clothes _____ every week.
3 We eat Spanish _____ a lot.

2 Choose the correct answer.

1 We _____ our teeth every day.
   a clean   b get
2 I _____ my homework in the afternoon.
   a do   b go
3 What time do you _____ up?
   a do   b get
4 They _____ breakfast in the morning.
   a have   b go
5 You _____ a shower at seven o'clock.
   a do   b have
6 We _____ television for one hour.
   a watch   b have
7 I _____ to school at eight o'clock.
   a have   b go
8 They _____ to bed early.
   a go   b do

3 Look at the pictures and complete the questions.

clean your teeth   get up   go to school
go to bed   have a shower   watch television

1 When do you *clean your teeth*?

4 Do you _____ _____ a lot?

2 What time do you _____?

5 When do you _____?

3 Where do you _____?

6 What time do you _____?

4 Complete the paragraph with these words.

bed   clean   drink   do   food   get   go
have   magazine   paint   shower

New   Reply

I always ¹ *get* up at seven o'clock. I usually
² _____ my teeth and have a ³ _____ . I
always ⁴ _____ breakfast and sometimes I
⁵ _____ orange juice. I ⁶ _____ to school
early. I love school. My favourite ⁷ _____ is
spaghetti. After school I sometimes draw and
⁸ _____ in my bedroom. I often ⁹ _____ my
homework at six o'clock. I usually read a
¹⁰ _____ at eight o'clock and I go to ¹¹ _____
at nine o'clock.

Grammar

5 Put the adverbs in order.

always   often   never   sometimes   ~~usually~~

	✔	✔	✔	✔	✔
usually	✔	✔	✔	✔	
	✔	✔	✔		
	✔	✔			
	✘				

6 Complete the paragraph with *always*, *usually*, *often*, *sometimes* or *never*.

I'm Jason and I've got two pets, Fluffy and Rex. Fluffy is a cat and Rex is a dog. We ¹ *sometimes* (✔✔) sit on a chair in the living room and watch TV programmes. Fluffy ² _____ (✔✔✔) sleeps on the chair. She ³ _____ (✘) plays with the dog. Fluffy and Rex are ⁴ _____ (✔✔✔✔) hungry. Fluffy ⁵ _____ (✔✔✔) washes after she eats. Rex ⁶ _____ (✔✔) plays with his toys. His favourite toy is his ball. He ⁷ _____ (✔✔✔) plays with it in the garden. We ⁸ _____ (✔✔✔✔) have a great time.

7 Circle the correct words.
1 My grandfather *don't* / *(doesn't)* get up early.
2 *Do* / *Does* you have a pet?
3 Who *goes* / *go* to school at nine o'clock?
4 What time *does* / *do* Anna go to bed?
5 *Do* / *Does* they have breakfast at half past seven?
6 *Does* / *Do* we have homework today?
7 *Do* / *Does* your school start at eight o'clock?

8 Write the sentences in the negative.
1 She likes chocolate ice cream.
   She doesn't like chocolate ice cream.
2 My father reads books.
   _____.
3 They speak English.
   _____.
4 My digital camera takes good photos.
   _____.
5 I have a pet dog.
   _____.
6 We ride our bikes to school.
   _____.
7 You go to bed at ten o'clock.
   _____.

9 Write questions and short answers.
1 always / Lea / get up / at half past seven / Does (✘)
   Does Lea always get up at half past seven?
   No, she doesn't.
2 Colin / have / usually / breakfast / Does (✔)
   _____?
   _____.
3 you / start / at half past eight / school / Do (✔)
   _____?
   _____.
4 they / go / Do / to bed / at nine o'clock (✘)
   _____?
   _____.
5 do / after school / her homework / Susie / Does (✔)
   _____?
   _____.
6 study / Do / we / English / always (✘)
   _____?
   _____.
7 the bird / have / every day / Does / food (✔)
   _____?
   _____.

3c Cosmic world

Vocabulary

1 Read the sentences and circle *True* or *False*.

1. Surya lives in India and her house is near the river. She always goes to school by boat on the river.
   - a Surya walks to school. True / **False**
   - b She lives on a houseboat. True / False

2. Craig lives in the desert in Australia. He stays at home and has lessons on the Internet.
   - a Craig doesn't go to school. True / False
   - b He hasn't got lessons. True / False

3. William lives in the Congo. He walks to school through the forest with his brother.
   - a William isn't from Australia. True / False
   - b His brother doesn't go to school. True / False

2 Match the pictures to the countries in Exercise 1.

A India
B the Congo
C Australia

3 Complete the words.

1. by boat (yb abto)
2. d _ _ _ _ _ _ (sdetre)
3. f _ _ _ _ _ _ (rsefto)
4. r _ _ _ _ _ (rveir)
5. b _ _ _ _ (yb sbu)
6. s _ _ _ _ _ _ (psrpeu)

4 Look at the pictures and complete the sentences.

1 'How do you get to school?' 'By bus.'

4 They have _____ at seven o'clock.

2 He goes to school _____.

5 She walks to school through the _____.

3 'Where does he live?' 'He lives in the _____.'

6 He lives near a _____.

5 Complete the sentences with *in*, *at*, *on* and *every*.

1. Gavin listens to music *in* the afternoon.
2. Sakis has a shower _____ the evening.
3. We watch TV _____ the weekend.
4. They go to bed _____ half past nine.
5. The students do their homework _____ day.
6. _____ Saturdays I go to the cinema.
7. Dad goes out with his friends _____ night.
8. We go to our grandparents' house _____ Sundays.

Grammar

6 Match the subject and object pronouns.

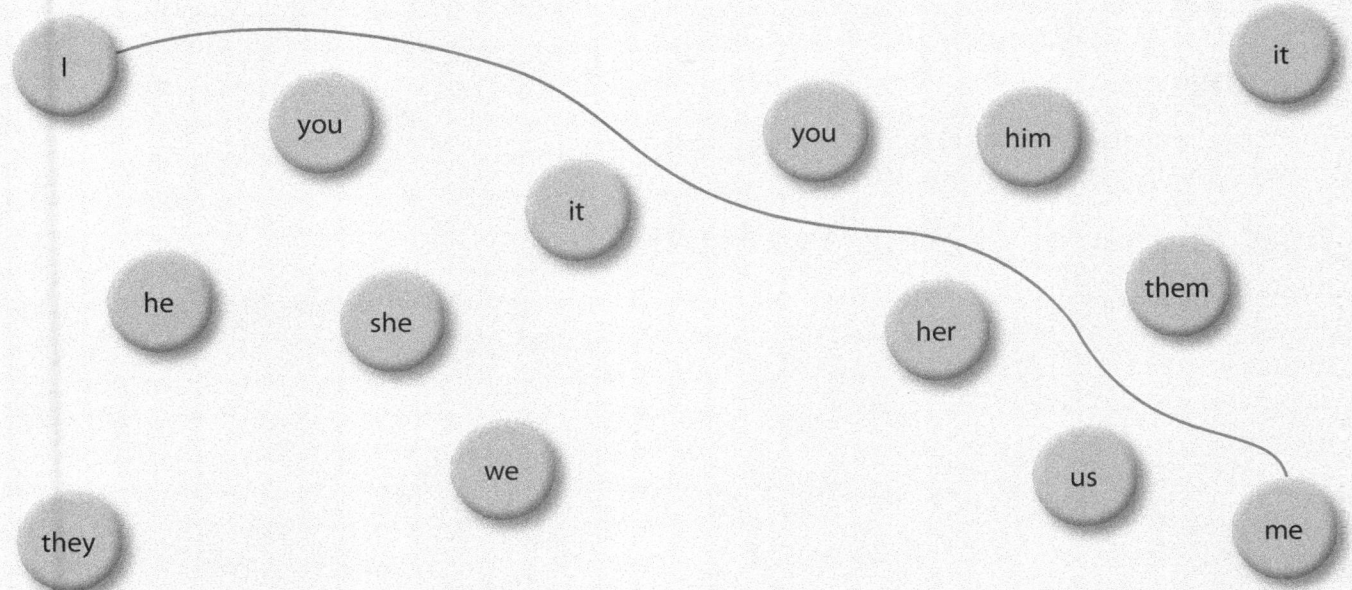

7 Circle the correct word.
1. Mum gives (me) / I supper at eight o'clock.
2. Our new school is great! We really like *it / its*.
3. Fiona, can I make *your / you* some spaghetti?
4. Here's my phone number. Please call *my / me* in the afternoon.
5. We're in the house. Come and find *we / us*!
6. These are my new friends. Come and meet *them / they*.
7. John's a new boy at school. Judy really likes *his / him*.
8. There's Jane. I see *she / her* every day.

8 Complete the sentences with *me, you, him, her, it, us* and *them*.
1. The dog is hungry. Give *it* some food.
2. I'm three years old in this photo. Can you see _____?
3. Mary's a nice girl. John likes _____.
4. Chris is my friend. I play football with _____ every weekend.
5. They're in Australia. Don't call _____ now. It's late.
6. We're at the park. Come and play a game with _____.
7. Mum, I love _____.

9 Complete the sentences. Use *because* and these words.

> ~~he likes it~~   I go to bed early   it's easy
> he's from France   she loves it
> they go to school   there isn't a bus

1. He often eats fish *because he likes it*.
2. My friend speaks French _____.
3. I like English _____.
4. Mum often eats chocolate _____.
5. They get up early on Monday morning _____.
6. I don't go out at twelve o'clock at night _____.
7. We walk to school _____.

29

Skills 2

Reading

1 Read the texts. Then label the pictures *Katy and friends*, *Mike and his sister* or *Sally and friends*.

What do they do in their free time?

1 Sally and friends

2 _____

3 _____

Katy loves television! She watches ¹it in her bedroom every day, but she always does her homework first. She usually goes out with her friends on Saturdays. They go to the shops and look at nice clothes and shoes. Sometimes they buy a lot of things! After shopping, they have lunch. They usually have spaghetti and drink lemonade. They love Italian food!

In their free time, Mike and ²_____ friends often play computer games. They're all very good players. Mike plays sports games and car games on his computer, but he doesn't always play computer games. He also does puzzles and he plays chess. Mike has got a sister. Her name's Mary. She watches ³_____ when he plays chess with his friends. They play every evening after school.

Sally collects something very strange ... dogs! In her town, there are a lot of dogs. They haven't got homes or families. They live in the park. Every day after school, Sally goes to the park and gives ⁴_____ food and water. Sometimes her friends help ⁵_____ because they like animals too. At the weekend, Sally and her friends ride their bikes into town. They usually go to the cinema.

2 Complete the texts with these words.

> her   him   his   ~~it~~   them

3 Complete the sentences with Katy, Mike or Sally.
1 *Katy* goes to the shops.
2 _____ does puzzles.
3 _____ goes to the cinema.
4 _____ eats spaghetti.
5 _____ loves animals.
6 _____ plays computer games.

4 Answer the questions.
1 Does Mike like car games?
   Yes, he does.
2 Does Katy go to the shops on Fridays?
   _____
3 Does Mike's sister play chess?
   _____
4 Does Sally help animals?
   _____
5 Does Katy always buy clothes?
   _____
6 Do Sally's friends play computer games?
   _____

Writing

5 Circle the correct word.
1 I like hamsters (and) / but parrots.
2 Do you go out with friends *but / or* your sisters?
3 I do puzzles *or / because* I like them.
4 I watch TV *and / but* I don't play computer games.
5 Jenny doesn't go to the cinema *but / and* she watches films on television.
6 Tim hasn't got a dog *or / and* a cat.

6 Complete the table about your free time. What do you? When you do it? Why do you like it?

What?
_____
_____
When?
_____
_____
Why?
_____
_____

7 Write about your free time. Use the ideas from Exercise 6. Remember to use time expressions like *in the morning* and *on Mondays*.

My free time activities

In my free time, I _____

_____

and _____.

I _____

(time expression) and I _____

_____

(time expression).

I like _____

because _____.

And I like _____

because _____.

31

Review 3

Vocabulary

1 Complete the sentences with free time words.

1 I *do puzzles*.
2 I take _____.
3 I ride _____.
4 I play _____.
5 I collect _____.
6 I go out with _____.

2 Circle the correct words.

I do a lot of things. I ¹ go /(get up) at seven o'clock in the morning. I ² have / do a shower and I ³ go / have breakfast at half past seven. Then I ⁴ take / go to school. After school I ⁵ watch / play television for an hour. I ⁶ do / have my homework. Then I ⁷ have / take supper. I ⁸ clean / get my teeth. Then I ⁹ have / go to bed.

3 Choose the correct answers.

1 We don't go to school _____ the weekend.
   (a) at   b in
2 I often go out with my friends _____ the afternoon.
   a in   b on
3 We have a big breakfast _____ Sunday.
   a at   b every
4 We don't go to school _____ Saturdays.
   a on   b in
5 Sharon goes to bed _____ nine o'clock.
   a in   b at
6 I always have breakfast _____ the morning.
   a at   b in

4 Write the words.

1 *famous*   mofuas
2 _____   gziamnae
3 _____   perpus
4 _____   ndeolmae
5 _____   vreir

Grammar

5 Circle the correct words.

1 How often do you (listen)/ listens to music?
2 My kitten *doesn't like / don't like* water.
3 These oranges *taste / tastes* nice.
4 Sam *isn't / doesn't* eat meat.
5 I *don't / am not* play the piano.
6 We *watches / watch* sports on television every Sunday.
7 The football game *starts / start* at eight o'clock.
8 They *doesn't / don't* live in China.

6 Write the sentences with never (X), sometimes (✓✓), often (✓✓✓), usually (✓✓✓✓) or always (✓✓✓✓✓).

1 Jane / go to bed / late on Saturdays (✓✓)
   Jane sometimes goes to bed late on Saturdays.
2 My kitten / plays / in the morning (✓✓✓✓✓)
   _____.
3 My friend and I / watch / football on television (✓✓✓)
   _____
   _____.
4 I / am / hungry / at half past two (✓✓✓✓)
   _____
   _____.
5 We / go to school / on Sunday (X)
   _____
   _____.

7 Tick (✓) the correct questions. Put a cross (X) next to the wrong questions.

1 Does your brother like chess? ✓
2 Do your friends plays computer games? ☐
3 Do you listens to music? ☐
4 Do your cousins collect stamps? ☐
5 Does your granny plays the piano? ☐
6 Does your kitten sleep all day? ☐

8 Complete the sentences with *me, you, her, him, it, us* or *them*.

1 There's Nick. Do you know *him*?
2 'Do you want to go out this weekend?' 'OK, call _____ on Saturday.'
3 These sandwiches are good. What's in _____?
4 I know _____. You're in my class.
5 We're at a party in this photo. Look at _____.
6 Here's my new computer game. Let's play _____?
7 He likes _____. What's her name?

9 Complete the blog.

My Cosmic Blog! ⊠

Tell us about your free-time activities.

What do you do in your free time?

In my free time, I always _____
_____
_____.

I sometimes, _____
_____
_____.

I don't _____,
and I never _____
_____.

Colour the Stars

0-8 mistakes:
Brilliant work!

9-15 mistakes:
Great work!

More than 15 mistakes:
Good try. Revise and try again!

4a Pet food

Vocabulary

1 Look at the pictures and circle the correct words.

 There are some pet *thieves* / *food* in this town. They *shut up* / *steal* expensive pets.

 *Let's stop* / *Get out of the way* here. I'd like some bananas and nuts for Echo.

 How much chocolate do you eat? It's *bad* / *sure* for your teeth.

 They've got a lot of *pet food* / *nuts*.

 Be quiet and *be careful* / *get out* of the way!

2 Complete the sentences with these words.

> bad for   Get out of the way   nuts
> pet food   steal   thief

1 My dad eats some *nuts* every day. He loves them.
2 Sweets and chocolate are _____ you.
3 Help! That _____ has got my bag!
4 I hate kids! _____, child!
5 Those men _____ expensive cars.
6 I'd like some _____ for my dog, Rusty.

3 Circle the odd one out.

1 oranges   cereal   *water*
2 milk   bread   chips
3 fruit   vegetables butter
4 fish   salad   crisps
5 biscuits   cheese   eggs
6 meat   sandwich   chicken

4 Look at the pictures and complete the crossword puzzle.

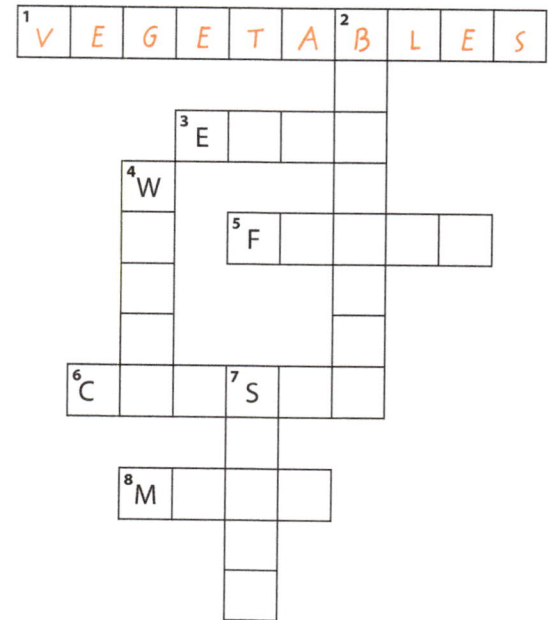

Grammar

5 Choose the correct answers.

1 Do you like white or brown _____ bread?
  a – (circled)   b a
2 There are five _____ on the table.
  a tomato   b tomatoes
3 He usually has two _____ and milk after school.
  a biscuits   b biscuit
4 There are _____ oranges in the bag.
  a three   b a
5 Meat _____ red.
  a are   b is
6 Is _____ milk bad for you?
  a –   b a

6 Complete the lists with these words.

> ~~apple~~ biscuit bread butter cheese
> chocolate crisp meat milk nut
> orange sweet

Countable
1 apple
2 _____
3 _____
4 _____
5 _____
6 _____

Uncountable
7 _____
8 _____
9 _____
10 _____
11 _____
12 _____

7 Circle the correct words.

A: Let's make breakfast.
B: Have we got ¹ some / **any** cereal?
A: No, we haven't got ² some / any cereal, but we've got ³ some / any eggs.
A: Have we got ⁴ some / any bread and cheese?
B: Yes, we have. Let's make eggs and ⁵ some / any sandwiches.
A: Have we got ⁶ some / any milk?
B: No, we haven't, but there are ⁷ some / any oranges. Let's make ⁸ some / any orange juice.
A: Great, I love orange juice!

8 Read and complete with *some* or *any*.

Hello, and welcome to your favourite TV programme: Kids in the Kitchen!

Have you got ¹ any free time after school? Of course you have! Are you hungry? Yes? Have you got ² _____ fruit? Well, let's make a fruit salad. It's very easy. Just get ³ _____ apples, ⁴ _____ oranges and ⁵ _____ bananas. Wash the apples with ⁶ _____ water. Cut all the fruit with a knife. Have you got ⁷ _____ nuts? You have? Great! Put ⁸ _____ nuts on the fruit. Your fruit salad is ready!

4b Your world

Vocabulary

1 Match.

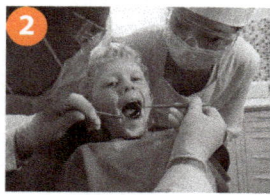

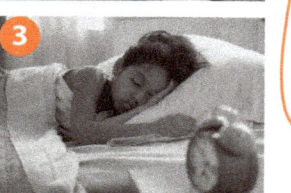

A Healthy teeth
B Sleep
C Exercise
D Healthy food

2 Find and write the words.

vsnexerciseotphourswbimealsminsidethyearvudentistfsaoutsideqneedy

1 exercise
2 _____
3 _____
4 _____
5 _____
6 _____
7 _____
8 _____

3 Complete the sentences with these words.

> dentist   exercise   hours   inside
> meal   outside   year

1 Sleep eight *hours* every night.
2 Always clean your teeth and visit the _____.
3 It's a beautiful day. Let's play _____.
4 _____ is good for you.
5 How many days are in a year? '_____'.
6 Which is your favourite _____? Breakfast, lunch or dinner?
7 It's really cold today. Let's stay _____ and play computer games.

4 Complete the crossword puzzle.

```
        ¹D     ²P
    ³M   E
        N
⁴H  ⁵E   T
        I
        S
        ⁶T
        
⁷S
```

ACROSS

3 In June and July, we eat our _____ on the balcony.
4 Fruit and vegetables are _____ food.
6 Have you got any health _____ for me?
7 We need eight hours _____ every night.

DOWN

1 How many times do you go to the _____ every year?
2 Do you _____ sport three times every week?
5 We need some _____ every day.

36

Grammar

5 Circle the correct words. Then write *True* (T) or *False* (F) for you.

1 How *much* / *many* exercise do you do every week?
   I exercise four times a week.

2 How *much* / *many* meals do you eat every day?
   I eat three meals: breakfast, lunch and dinner.

3 How *much* / *many* computer games have you got?
   I have got a lot of computer games.

4 How *much* / *many* hours do you sleep every night?
   I sleep about nine hours every night.

5 How *much* / *many* water do you drink every day?
   I don't drink any water.

6 How *much* / *many* sweets do you eat every day?
   I don't eat sweets every day.

6 Complete the sentences with *How much* or *How many*.

1 *How much* milk do you drink every day?
2 _____ apples does Rob take to school?
3 _____ orange juice do you want?
4 _____ chocolate do they eat?
5 _____ sandwiches has she got?
6 _____ pet food does the cat eat?
7 _____ times do you play outside every week?
8 _____ fruit do you eat every week?

7 Circle the correct words.

1 There's *a lot of* / *a few* food on my plate.
2 Take *a few* / *a little* apples with you.
3 We eat *a little* / *a lot of* vegetables.
4 Here's *a little* / *a few* chocolate.
5 The programme starts in *a little* / *a few* minutes.
6 There are *a lot of* / *a little* people at the dentist's.
7 I'd like *a little* / *a few* butter on my bread.
8 We play outside *a little* / *a few* hours each day.

8 Look at the pictures and complete the sentences with *a lot of*, *a few* or *a little*.

1 That's *a lot of* chocolate! Don't eat it all.

2 Here are _____ nuts for Echo. He loves them.

3 There's _____ milk in the glass.

4 There's _____ fruit in the bowl.

5 We've got _____ eggs.

6 There's only _____ cheese.

4c Cosmic world

Vocabulary

1 Match.

A

Don't watch television. Stay in a dark room and drink a lot of water.

B

Start the day with a healthy breakfast. Eat some porridge or a fruit 'smoothie'.

C

Drink hot lemon juice with honey and garlic.

1 I've got a cold. C
2 I've got a headache. ☐
3 I'm sleepy in the mornings. ☐

2 Circle the correct words.

1
salt / garlic

4
yoghurt / salt

2
juice / porridge

5
garlic / porridge

3
honey / juice

6
honey / yoghurt

3 Put the letters in order and complete the sentences.

1 My brother is a *doctor*. (todroc)
2 She doesn't feel well. She feels _____. (cksi)
3 The _____ has got some water for you. (srnue)
4 The little boy has got _____. (mtuym hace)
5 Anna's got a _____ on her hand. (tuc)
6 Here's some lemon juice with honey. You've got a _____. (dolc)
7 Frank's leg _____. (utrhs)
8 You've got a _____. Stay in a dark room. (ecahehda)

4 Find and write the food and health words.

Y O G H U R T E X W R H
K K E O O N U R S E T E
C K G N U B S Q D T R A
C Z A E G A G I I J D D
O Q R Y L R A D L U R A
L A E L R S R Q R I M C
D A I E S A L T O C M H
R A P O R R I D G E P E
C W F L D O C T O R M J

1 yoghurt
2 _____
3 _____
4 _____
5 _____
6 _____
7 _____
8 _____
9 _____
10 _____

Grammar

5 Circle the correct answers.

1 'My leg hurts.' '_____ on a chair.'
   a Let's sit
   (b) Sit
2 _____ a lot of sweets.
   a Don't eat
   b To eat
3 'I've got a headache.' '_____ in a dark room.'
   a Don't stay
   b Stay
4 'I've got a cold.' '_____ a hot lemon drink.'
   a Let's make
   b You make
5 Let's _____ a healthy breakfast.
   a eat
   b don't eat
6 _____ the dentist every six months.
   a To visit
   b Visit
7 _____! We need strawberries for the smoothies.
   a Don't forget
   b Forget
8 _____ your teeth every day.
   a Let's clean
   b Clean

6 Write the negative imperatives.

1 Look!
   Don't look!
2 Add salt.
   _____.
3 Make a hot drink.
   _____.
4 Run!
   _____!
5 Drink coffee.
   _____.
6 Eat lots of chocolate.
   _____.

7 Write the sentences in Exercise 6 using Let's.

1 *Let's look!*
2 _____.
3 _____.
4 _____!
5 _____.
6 _____.

8 Circle the correct words.

My grandmother's tip for a hurt leg

1 (First) / After that get some garlic.
2 Finally / Then put it in a bag.
3 After that / First put the bag on the hurt leg and leave it on for 2 hours.
4 Finally / Then, remove the bag and wash your leg.

9 Complete the sentences. Use After that, First, Finally, or Then.

French toast for breakfast!

First, get some bread, milk and eggs. 2 _____ mix the milk and eggs. 3 _____, put the bread in the milk and eggs. Add a little salt. 4 _____, cook the bread for a few minutes and eat hot. French toast is delicious with strawberries.

Review 4

Vocabulary

1 Circle the correct words.

cereal / biscuits (cereal circled)

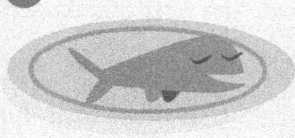
crisps / chips

meat / fish

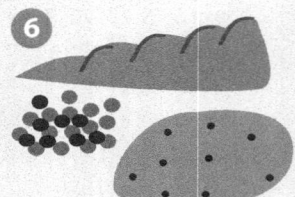
vegetables / fruit

milk / water

sandwich / bread

cheese / chicken

eggs / butter

2 Write the correct word.

| garlic   honey   juice   porridge |
| salt   ~~yoghurt~~ |

1 It's from milk.   yoghurt
2 It's sweet.   _____
3 We drink this.   _____
4 Crisps have got lots of this.   _____
5 It's a vegetable.   _____
6 It's cereal and hot milk.   _____

3 Match.

1 I've got a   A sick.
2 I've got a tummy   B on my dog's leg.
3 Look! There's a cut C headache.
4 Ouch! My hand   D a cold.
5 Atchoo! I've got   E hurts.
6 I feel   F ache.

(1 matched to C)

4 Complete the sentences.

1 How often do you eat *meat*? (team)
2 Have we got any _____? (redab)
3 How many _____ are there in the bag? (narosge)
4 There aren't many _____. (gseg)
5 There's a lot of _____ in French food. (utbetr)

Grammar

5 Choose the correct answers.

1 I'd like _____ bread, please.
   a some (circled)
   b any
2 Have you got _____ bananas?
   a some
   b any
3 How _____ money is in your pocket?
   a much
   b many
4 How _____ biscuits do you eat every day?
   a much
   b many
5 You have got _____ keys.
   a a lot of
   b a little
6 There is _____ water in the bottle.
   a some
   b a few
7 _____ chocolate isn't bad for you.
   a A few
   b A little

6 Complete each sentence with one word.
1 I'd like *some* biscuits, please.
2 There are a _____ oranges on the table.
3 How _____ eggs do we need for the cake?
4 There's only a _____ juice in the glass.
5 I haven't got _____ milk for my cereal.
6 How _____ water is in the bottle?
7 Has Dina got _____ crisps?
8 There are a _____ of bikes in the garden.

7 Match the sentences.
1 It's hot.
2 My leg hurts.
3 We're late for school.
4 I've got a new CD.
5 I'm hungry.
6 These chips aren't nice.

A Add a little salt.
B Let's listen to it.
C Drink some cold water.
D See the doctor.
E Let's run!
F Eat some fruit.

8 Complete the sentences with the imperative of these verbs in the affirmative or negative.

eat   go   have   listen   play   ride

1 'I'm bored.' '*Play* a computer game.'
2 _____ your bike in the living room!
3 'I'm hungry.' '_____ a sandwich.'
4 'My tooth hurts.' '_____ to the dentist.'
5 'I'm dirty.' '_____ a shower.'
6 'This music is great. _____ to it.'

9 Complete the blog.

My Cosmic Blog!

Tell us how you stay healthy.

I am healthy because every day, I
_____.

I also, _____.

I don't often
_____
and I never
_____.

Colour the Stars

0-8 mistakes:
Brilliant work!

9-15 mistakes:
Great work!

More than 15 mistakes:
Good try. Revise and try again!

41

5a Tiny is missing!

Vocabulary

1 Look at the pictures and read the sentences. Write *True* (T) or *False* (F).

Alex and Ellie are playing volleyball. **T**

Echo is sitting on the towel. ☐

The man and woman are walking to the car park. ☐

Alex is riding his bike and Ellie is taking a photo. ☐

Ellie and Alex have got a photo of the pet thieves. ☐

2 Match.

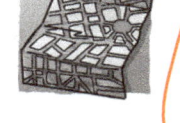

A look for
B drive
C magnifying glass
D follow
E map
F car park

3 Circle the correct words.

1 Let's go (swimming) / *karate* in the river.
2 The two boys are playing *windsurfing* / *tennis* on the grass.
3 Have you got a bike? Let's go *athletics* / *cycling*.
4 I've got a ball. Let's play *gymnastics* / *basketball*.
5 We don't play *volleyball* / *diving* in the water.
6 We do *water-skiing* / *tennis* in this river.

4 Complete the crossword puzzle.

ACROSS

2 Where is the zoo? Let's look at the _____ .
4 You do _____ , swimming and water-skiing in the water.
6 Look at those people. Let's _____ them.
8 You wear a white uniform for _____ .
9 You play _____ and basketball with a ball.

DOWN

1 We're putting the car in the *car park*.
3 Things look big with a _____ .
5 My granny doesn't _____ a car.
7 Where's Bianca? Let's _____ her.

Grammar

5 Look at the picture and circle the correct answers.

1 A girl _____ a bike.
   a isn't riding
   b is riding ✓
2 A man and a woman _____ a picnic.
   a are having
   b aren't having
3 The dog _____.
   a isn't sleeping
   b is sleeping
4 A boy and a girl _____ volleyball.
   a are playing
   b aren't playing
5 A man _____ photos.
   a isn't taking
   b is taking
6 Three children _____ in the river.
   a are windsurfing.
   b aren't windsurfing

6 Circle the correct words.
1 I *am* / *do* drinking a fruit smoothie. It's good.
2 You *isn't* / *aren't* taking photos.
3 Gran *is* / *are* watching her favourite television programme.
4 Mum and Dad *isn't* / *aren't* looking for me.
5 He *aren't* / *isn't* playing volleyball.
6 The cat *isn't* / *aren't* sitting on the map.
7 I *am not* / *aren't* going to bed.
8 We *is* / *are* going to our friend's birthday party.

7 Complete the sentences. Use these words in the present continuous.

> drive   lie   ~~play~~   ride   swim   take

1 I *am playing* volleyball with Sarah.
2 You _____ in the river with Steve and Mike.
3 James _____ a photo with his digital camera.
4 Poppy _____ her bike in the garden.
5 The dog _____ on the grass.
6 Mum and Dad _____ their cars.

8 Write these sentences in the negative.
1 I am writing an e-mail.
   I am not writing an e-mail.
2 You are reading a comic.
   _____.
3 Pat is having a shower.
   _____.
4 Harry is riding a bike.
   _____.
5 We are playing basketball.
   _____.
6 Charlie and Jo are studying.
   _____.
7 The hamster is lying on my bed.
   _____.

5b Your world

Vocabulary

1 Find the words and complete the sentences.

P	T	U	S	E	N	G	Q	I	P
R	V	A	J	V	R	R	A	Q	L
O	J	F	E	O	T	W	S	T	B
J	S	O	J	R	F	M	A	P	L
E	B	E	C	T	G	T	F	U	N
C	C	D	S	M	T	E	J	V	A
T	E	A	C	H	E	R	T	G	G
K	T	T	D	U	M	M	E	C	Q

1 How many times do you *use* your mobile phone every day?
2 This _____ we're studying India in Geography.
3 Cara's doing a _____ on computers this month.
4 Our new _____ is always late.
5 Mr Trainer's Art class is great _____ .

2 Match.

 1
 2
 3
 4
 5
 6
 7
 8

A Computer Studies
B Drama
C Geography
D Physical Education
E Science
F History
G Maths
H Art

3 Read the dialogue and write the subjects in the timetable.

Jason: Let's look at our subjects for this year. First, when have we got English?
Holly: It's Lesson 2 every Monday, Wednesday and Friday. And when have we got Science?
Jason: We do Science twice a week. It's Lessons 1 and 2 on Tuesdays and Thursdays. Then we've got Maths. It's Lesson 3 every day. When have we got History?
Holly: That's twice a week. It's Lesson 4 on Tuesdays and Thursdays. After that we've got Computer Studies. That's Lesson 5. Have we got French this year?
Jason: Let's see. Yes, it's Lessons 4 and 5 on Mondays. Hey, we've only got Art once a week. It's Lesson 1 on a Friday.
Holly: I know! But we've got PE four times a week!

	Monday	Tuesday	Wednesday	Thursday	Friday
Lesson 1	Geography	Science	Geography	2 _____	3 _____
Lesson 2	¹ *English*		English		English
Lesson 3	Maths	4 _____	Maths	Maths	5 _____
Lesson 4	French	6 _____	PE	History	PE
Lesson 5	7 _____	Computer Studies	PE	8 _____	PE

4 Complete the sentences.

1 I'm studying *French* today. (rnheFc)
2 My favourite sport is gymnastics. It's great _____ . (unf)
3 'Why are you looking at the map?' 'I'm doing a _____ for Geography.' (ojrpetc)
4 We've got a lovely _____ called Miss White. (ehracte)
5 Simon does _____ on Wednesdays and Fridays. (rmaDa)
6 My favourite subject is _____ . (hilcPays dctiEnuao)
7 Do you like _____ ? (neScci)

Grammar

5 Match the questions to the answers.

1 What are Tina and Alex doing?
2 Is Jane painting a picture?
3 Are you writing an e-mail?
4 What are they eating?
5 Where are we going?
6 Why are you playing basketball?
7 Is David playing his new computer game?
8 Is the dog lying in the garden?

A No, she isn't. She's doing her homework.
B Because its our favourite sport.
C They're taking photos for their school project.
D Yes, he is. It's great fun!
E We're going to Jim's school.
F No, it isn't. It's playing with the ball.
G They're eating spaghetti.
H Yes, I am. I'm writing to my friend in England.

6 Circle the correct words.

1 What *are you doing* / *do you do* at the moment?
2 'Why *she is* / *is she* studying?' 'She's got a test tomorrow.'
3 'Where *are you* / *do you* going?' 'I'm going to karate.'
4 Are they *talking* / *talk* to a volleyball player?
5 '*Is it* / *It is* moving?' 'No, it isn't.'
6 What *they writing* / *are they writing* today?
7 '*Are we* / *Are* listening to the teacher?' 'Yes, we are!'

7 Write questions. Use these words.

1 are / e-mail / writing / you / Why / an
   Why are you writing an e-mail?
2 doing / he / What / is
   _____?
3 subjects / many / studying / How / you / are
   _____?
4 she / painting / Is
   _____?
5 French / they / speaking / or / Are / Spanish
   _____?
6 now / reading / are / you / What
   _____?
7 doing / project / they / Are / a
   _____?
8 Am / drawing / I / picture / nice / a
   _____?

8 Look at the picture and answer the questions. Use short answers.

1 Is the teacher watching the students?
   No, she isn't.
2 Is a boy eating an orange?
   _____.
3 Are all the children sitting?
   _____.
4 Is a boy sleeping?
   _____.
5 Is a girl drawing on her desk?
   _____.
6 Are the children using their laptops?
   _____.
7 Are some children playing?
   _____.
8 Is a boy writing on the board?
   _____.

45

5c Cosmic world

Vocabulary

1 Label the pictures.

Drama   Art   ~~Sport~~

1 Sport

2

3

2 Choose the correct answers.

1 Our Drama teacher is also _____.
 a) an actor
 b a gym

2 Let's play outside in the _____.
 a playground
 b coach

3 We have a _____ from lessons at half past eleven.
 a play
 b break

4 Our _____ teaches us football and basketball.
 a actor
 b coach

5 We do sport inside in the _____ at our school.
 a gym
 b playground

6 Jack and Isabelle are doing a _____. They sing and dance in it.
 a break
 b play

3 Complete the crossword puzzle.

		¹C		
²P	³A	⁴G	O	
			A	
			C	
			H	
⁵B				

ACROSS
2 Children play outside in the _____ at school.
5 Lessons stop and everyone has a _____.

DOWN
1 A _____ teaches sports.
2 We are seeing a _____ at the theatre.
3 An _____ is in films, television programmes or plays.
4 You do sports in a _____.

4 Complete the blog with these words.

actor   break   coach   ~~Drama~~   dancing
drawing   gym   play

 New   Reply

Hi! My name is Matt. My school is in Australia. I like ¹ *Drama* because I love singing and ² _____. We do a ³ _____ at the end of every term in my school. This term we're doing Peter Pan. I'm an ⁴ _____ in it. I don't like Art because I'm not very good at ⁵ _____ or painting. But I love sport. The ⁶ _____ is my favourite teacher. My friends and I play Brazilian football in the school ⁷ _____. When we've got a ⁸ _____ we sometimes play volleyball outside in the playground.

46

Grammar

5 Circle the correct words.
1 What *do you do* / *are you doing* right now?
2 *I'm not having* / *I don't have* Drama at my school.
3 We usually *play* / *are playing* in the playground in the break.
4 They *don't swim* / *aren't swimming* today. It's cold.
5 *Do you go* / *Are you going* to the cinema every week?
6 She never *eats* / *isn't eating* fish because she doesn't like it.
7 *I'm doing* / *I do* my History project at the moment.
8 Tod goes to a football club *at the moment* / *on Sundays*.

6 Match the questions to the short answers.
1 Is he painting right now?
2 Does Mrs Choi write e-mails every day?
3 Does Mr Brown, the coach play Brazilian music?
4 Are the children doing a play this term?
5 Does school start at eight o'clock in England?
6 Are you playing in the playground now?

A No, she doesn't.
B Yes, they are.
C No, it doesn't.
D Yes, he is.
E No, I'm not.
F Yes, he does.

7 Complete the sentences with these words. Use the present simple (PS) or the present continuous (PC).

   eat   not have   speak   use   watch   work

1 I *don't watch* my favourite TV programme every day. PS
2 He _____ Spanish right now. PC
3 _____ you often _____ your laptop? PS
4 They _____ at the weekend. PS
5 We _____ lunch in the playground today. PC
6 She _____ a piano lesson at the moment. PC

8 Correct the sentences.
1 Patty plays tennis twice the week.   a
2 Look at those dogs. They be playing football! _____
3 That girl am windsurfing right now. She's very fast. _____
4 Sams taking some photos. _____
5 We are doing our homework at six o'clock every evening. _____
6 How many subjects do you studying at school? _____

9 Complete the paragraph. Use the present simple or the present continuous.

These children ¹ *go* (go) to an English school. They ² _____ (do) Maths, Science and English three times a week. They also ³ _____ (do) Art and Music. Their school always ⁴ _____ (start) at nine and ⁵ _____ (finish) at four. They usually ⁶ _____ (wear) uniforms, but today they ⁷ _____ (not wear) them. They ⁸ _____ (not have got) lessons today because it's Saturday. At the moment, they ⁹ _____ (not do) their homework. They ¹⁰ _____ (play) outside in a forest. ¹¹ _____ (they/have) lots of fun right now? Yes, they are. They ¹² _____ (love) weekends!

47

Reading

1 Read the texts and write the countries under the pictures.

Japanese people eat very healthy food. We eat a lot of fish, but only a little meat. Sometimes, we don't cook the fish! We eat a lot of vegetables. We make salads with lots of different vegetables. We don't eat much bread, but we eat a lot of rice. We always have some rice with our breakfast. In Japan, we sometimes have vegetables for breakfast. People from other countries think it's strange, but we don't. We love it! And it's good for us! We don't eat many biscuits or cakes. We eat a lot of fruit when we want something sweet. We are very healthy people!

In Germany, people love meat, bread and potatoes! Meat is our favourite food. We eat it for breakfast, lunch and supper. We always have bread with our meals. We make white and brown bread. People from other countries love German bread! We eat a lot of sandwiches too, and we put some meat and salad in them. We also like cheese, and we eat a lot of yoghurt. Germans also eat a lot of sweets and cakes. They are fantastic! We don't eat a lot of fresh fruit, but we make cakes and sweets with fruit like apples.

1 _____   2 _____

48

2 Complete the table. Put (✓) for food they eat a lot of or (✗) for food they eat a little of.

	Japan	Germany
fish	✓	✗
meat		
vegetables		
bread		
rice		
biscuits		
cakes		
fresh fruit		
cheese		
yoghurt		

3 Read the text again and answer the questions.

1 How much rice do they eat in Japan?
In Japan they eat a lot of rice.

2 How many cakes do they eat in Germany?
_____

3 What do they have for breakfast in Germany?
_____

4 What do they have for breakfast in Japan?
_____

5 Who don't eat bread?
_____

6 Who don't eat a lot of fresh fruit?
_____

4 Match.

1 I've got a lot of vegetables.
2 I've got some milk and some cereal.
3 I've got some bread and some cheese.
4 I've got some chicken and some chips.
5 I've got a few strawberries and some milk.

A I'm making a sandwich.
B I'm making a smoothie.
C I'm making a salad.
D I'm eating dinner.
E I'm having breakfast.

Writing

5 Make a list of the food people eat in your country.
_____
_____
_____
_____
_____

6 Which food in Exercise 5 do you like? Tick.

7 Write about the food in your country.

Food we eat in my country

We eat a lot of _____
_____.

We also really like _____
_____.

People eat a lot of _____
in my country.

We don't eat a lot of _____
_____

because _____
_____.

We also don't eat _____
_____.

For breakfast we _____
_____.

For lunch we _____
_____.

For supper we _____
_____.

Review 5

Vocabulary

1 Write the sports.

basketball cycling diving gymnastics swimming volleyball

1 basketball
2 _____
3 _____
4 _____
5 _____
6 _____

2 Circle the correct answers.

What do you do in …

1 Art?
   (a) We draw and paint.   b We write emails.
2 Computer Studies?
   a We make computers.   b We use computers.
3 Drama?
   a We play chess.   b We act, sing and dance.
4 Geography?
   a We study countries.   b We sit on the beach.
5 Maths?
   a We do projects.   b We study numbers.
6 History?
   a We play football.
   b We learn about the past.

3 Look at the timetable and answer the questions.

1 What do you do on Monday?
   Maths, _____
2 What do you do on Tuesday?
   _____
3 What do you do on Wednesday?
   _____, _____
4 What do you do on Thursday?
   _____, _____
5 What do you do on Friday?
   _____

4 Circle the correct answer.

1 Every Monday, we (do) / are doing History.
2 Anna doesn't eat / isn't eating lunch today.
3 They are playing basketball now / every day.
4 Greek children don't wear / aren't wearing uniforms.
5 Tom studies / is studying at the moment.
6 I am always having / always have cereal.

Grammar

5 Complete the sentences with *am*, *'m not*, *is*, *isn't*, *are* or *aren't*.

1. Look at Mary! She *is* diving! (✓)
2. Lucy and Jason _____ drawing. (✗)
3. I _____ doing my homework now. (✓)
4. We _____ painting a nice picture. (✓)
5. Kevin _____ sleeping at the moment. (✗)
6. I _____ studying Maths today. (✗)
7. She _____ running to school. (✓)

6 Write about the pictures. Use the present continuous.

1. take a photo / draw a picture
   He is taking a photo. He isn't drawing a picture.

2. watch TV / read a comic
   He _____.

3. have supper / drink coffee
   They _____.

4. play the piano / ride a bike
   She _____.

7 Look at the photo and write questions and answers about Danny. Use the present continuous.

1. paint a picture?
   Is Danny painting a picture?
   No, he isn't.

2. use his laptop?
   _____

3. wear a tie
   _____

4. take photos?
   _____

5. brush his teeth?
   _____

8 Complete the blog.

My Cosmic Blog!

Tell us about your school and your favourite subjects.

I go to school from Monday to Friday. School starts at _____.
_____.

My favourite subjects are _____
_____.

Colour the Stars

0-8 mistakes:
Brilliant work!

9-15 mistakes:
Great work!

More than 15 mistakes:
Good try. Revise and try again!

6a The chase through town!

Vocabulary

1 Match the pictures to the sentences.

A The train station is on our left and the park is on our right.

B We're going past the cinema now, but I can't see them.

C OK. See you soon.

D You mustn't use your bell, Alex. There's a hospital in this street!

E Can you come and help us?

2 Look at the pictures and circle the correct words.

1 'Where is the hospital?' 'Go *straight on* / *past*!'
2 'Is there a supermarket here?' 'Yes, just *go past* / *turn left* into Bell Street.'
3 'Where's the cinema?' 'It's *on your right* / *go towards*.'
4 Look! He's *going past* / *turning left* Jacob's house.
5 Who's the man *on your right* / *in front of* the house?
6 That man is *going towards* / *in front* the phone.

3 Complete the crossword puzzle.

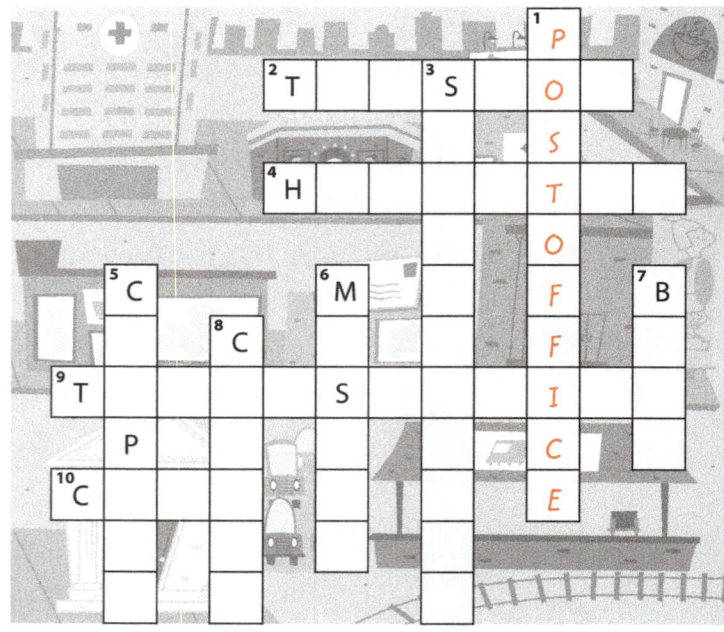

ACROSS
2 You buy presents for children here.
4 You go there when you're very sick.
9 You catch trains here.
10 People meet and drink coffee here.

DOWN
1 You send letters here.
3 You buy many things here.
5 You put cars in this.
6 There are many old and beautiful things here.
7 People put their money in this.
8 You watch films here.

4 Complete the sentences with these words.

café cinema front hospital right supermarket

1 We watch films at the *cinema* every Thursday.
2 There's a new toy shop in _____ of the train station.
3 'Where's the bank?' 'On your _____.'
4 Doctors and nurses usually work in a _____.
5 Let's have a coffee at this _____.
6 I'm going to the _____ for some milk.

52

Grammar

5 Circle the correct words.

George: Where ¹ *was / were* you last night?

Tony: I ² *was / were* at the cinema with Tim and Nicole.

George: ³ *Was / Were* John there too?

Tony: No, he ⁴ *wasn't / weren't*. There ⁵ *wasn't / weren't* many people.

George: ⁶ *Was / Were* the film good?

Tony: It ⁷ *was / were* great! It ⁸ *was / were* in 3D! How about you? ⁹ Where *was / were* you?

Tony: Oh! I ¹⁰ *was / were* at home with my cousins from England. They ¹¹ *was / were* here yesterday.

6 Look at Bob's holiday notes from last week. Read the sentences and write *True* (T) or *False* (F).

Monday 5th and Tuesday 6th	London a lot of rain dinner with Aunt Jane and Uncle Max on Tuesday evening
Wednesday 7th and Thursday 8th	Paris very nice hotel
Friday 9th and Saturday 10th	Rome great but cold great pizza for lunch
Sunday 11th	Athens sunny day a lot of people at the museum

1 There wasn't any rain in London.
2 Bob ate with his aunt and uncle on Tuesday evening.
3 He wasn't in Paris for two days.
4 The hotel in Paris was horrible.
5 Rome was great but the weather wasn't very nice.
6 The pizza was fantastic.
7 It's Monday 12th today. Bob wasn't in Athens yesterday.
8 A lot of people were at the museum but the weather was great.

7 Correct the *False* sentences from Exercise 6.

1 *There was a lot of rain in London.*

8 Write questions and answers. Use the verb *be* in the past simple.

1 be / they / at school yesterday? (✔)

   Were they at school yesterday? Yes, they were.

2 be / she / in the museum? (✘)

3 be / your birthday / a month ago? (✘)

4 be / it / cold last night? (✔)

5 be / there / a lot of people at the post office? (✘)

6 be / Alex / at a café / yesterday afternoon? (✔)

6b Your world

Vocabulary

1 Look at the pictures and circle the correct rule.

1 You must *shut gates* / *climb walls* after you.
2 You must *leave rubbish* / *use the bins* after picnics.
3 You mustn't *pick flowers* / *use the bins*.
4 You mustn't *write on trees* / *make fires*.
5 You mustn't *break fences* / *shut gates*.

2 Complete the sentences with these words.

> beautiful   go fishing   pick   ~~picnic~~
> rubbish   shut

1 Let's have a *picnic* in the forest.
2 What a _____ day! Let's go for a swim.
3 Please _____ the gate. The dog mustn't get out.
4 You mustn't _____ the flowers.
5 Dad and I _____ by the river. We love fish!
6 You can't leave your _____ here. Use a bin.

3 Find and write the countryside words.

```
M V A L L E Y M
I P A T H T X O
S F I E L D R U
L E U K G R B N
A N F O R E S T
N C L G A T E A
D E E C S T A I
H I L L S P F N
M F L O W E R S
```

1 *valley*   7 _____
2 _____   8 _____
3 _____   9 _____
4 _____   10 _____
5 _____   11 _____
6 _____   12 _____

4 Read and complete the paragraph.

Every year, we go to my grandparents' house in the ¹ *mountains* (aistmunon). It is very ² _____ (elabufitu) there. You can see the ³ _____ (eas) from the window in the living room. There is a ⁴ _____ (tpah) from the house to a ⁵ _____ (rsotfe). Every day we go for walks there and we usually ⁶ _____ (ckip) flowers for my grandmother. She loves flowers. We sometimes have a ⁷ _____ (npicci) in a ⁸ _____ (elfid) near the house. We sit on the ⁹ _____ (rsgas) and eat sandwiches and fruit and drink orange juice. We are always very careful. We never leave ¹⁰ _____ (bihrbus) and we always ¹¹ _____ (htus) the gate when we leave.

Grammar

5 Write *A* for Ability, and *P* for Permission.

1. Can I go to the cinema with my friends tonight?
   P
2. Look at you! You can ride a horse. ____
3. Sorry, you can't take photos in the museum. ____
4. Ellie can't ride a horse, but she can ride a bike. ____
5. The dog can walk on two legs. ____
6. Can we go camping this weekend? ____
7. Sorry, the children can't go into the field. ____
8. Sandra's only six, but she can windsurf. ____

6 Write *can* or *can't*.

1. Cats *can't* fly.
2. People ____ walk on water.
3. ____ I borrow your pencil please?
4. Wow, look at him! He ____ paint with his feet.
5. ____ we go to the playground before dinner?
6. 'Can computers tell jokes?' 'No, they ____.'
7. Look! She's really good.
   Grandma ____ dance well.
8. 'Can we go fishing later?' 'Yes, you ____.'
9. It's raining. We ____ make a fire outside.
10. I ____ swim in the sea, but I can't swim in a pool.

7 Circle the correct words.

1. You *must* / *mustn't* clean your teeth.
2. Children *must* / *mustn't* sleep at least eight hours a night.
3. You *must* / *mustn't* talk with your mouth full.
4. We *must* / *mustn't* give parrots chocolate.
5. We *must* / *mustn't* do exercise and be healthy.
6. The students *must* / *mustn't* make a lot of noise in class.
7. We *must* / *mustn't* clean our beaches.
8. Dogs *must* / *mustn't* play in the playground.

8 Write a class contract. Use *can*, *can't*, *must* or *mustn't*. Sometimes more than one answer is possible.

Class contract

Year 20 _____

1. We *musn't* eat or drink in class.
2. We _____ talk but we _____ shout.
3. We _____ play volleyball in the classroom.
4. We _____ do our homework.
5. We _____ play in the break.
6. We _____ eat and drink in the break.
7. We _____ steal other students' things.
8. We _____
   _____ (your own answer)

Your signature
_____

Your teacher's signature
_____

6c Cosmic world

Vocabulary

1 Match.

Town
Country

- A amazing museums
- B fantastic birds
- C very quiet
- D green fields
- E busy streets
- F famous paintings
- G small island
- H dirty and noisy

2 Find and write the words.

reboringmsdangerousopnoisyasdhungrykiodirtybmquiet

1 boring
2 _____
3 _____
4 _____
5 _____
6 _____

3 Write the words.

1 Not many people live in the country. (runycto)
2 We can see _____ in museums. They are usually very old. (tsaetus)
3 _____ live in green fields and they eat grass. (ehesp)
4 It isn't noisy here. It's _____. (etuiq)
5 A lot of people live in the _____. (wtno)
6 _____ are very small animals. (tcsnies)

4 Complete the text with these words.

amazing   boring   busy   noisy   small
penfriend   pop concert

21:42

Hi Gary! I'm with my ¹ penfriend David in London. We're at a
² _____ now. I can't talk to you on the phone because it's very
³ _____ in here because of the music. It is quite a ⁴ _____ theatre but there are a lot of people in it tonight. London is a very
⁵ _____ place because a lot of people live here. It's never
⁶ _____ in London because there are lots of things to do. It's
⁷ _____!

MENU   CONTACTS   BACK

<   >

1   2   3   4

Grammar

5 Write the adverbs of manner.

1 amazing → amazingly
2 brilliant →
3 quick →
4 slow →
5 horrible →
6 hungry →

6 Circle the correct words.

1 He plays the guitar *brilliant* / *brilliantly*.
2 She's speaking *quiet* / *quietly* because the baby is sleeping.
3 They're singing *horrible* / *horribly*.
4 I'm *hungry* / *hungrily*. Let's eat.
5 These children are *happy* / *happily*.
6 Talk *nice* / *nicely* to your teacher.
7 That was a *strange* / *strangely* dream.

7 Put a tick (✔) or a cross (✘).

1 He's riding his bike careful. ✘
2 Are you busily?
3 This boat is going very slowly.
4 You must walk quiet in the field.
5 The sheep are eating hungrily.
6 She's looking strangely at the statues.

8 Complete the sentences with the adverbs of manner.

> beautifully dangerously horribly noisily
> quickly slowly

1 They're driving dangerously. They mustn't do that.
2 Teachers must speak _____ to students.
3 She sings _____ but she can't dance very well.
4 They're talking very _____. They must be quiet in here.
5 We must leave _____ because we're late.
6 I paint _____, but my sister's an amazing artist.

9 Circle the correct words.

Dear Sophie,
My name's Eleni and I'm your ¹ new / old penfriend.
I live in Athens. It's a ² hungry / busy city with lots of people. It has got a lot of museums with ³ great / quiet statues. My favourite place is the Acropolis and there's a ⁴ famous / noisy temple, the Parthenon, at the top. You can see a picture with this letter. There are a lot of cars in Athens and the roads are very ⁵ dangerous / quiet.
I really love the Greek islands. I was on Santorini last summer. There were lots of ⁶ happy / amazing beaches. I'd like to go to Crete this year.
What about you?
Write soon,
Eleni

Vocabulary

1 Match.

A go past

B on your right

C go towards

D go straight on

E turn left

F in front of

2 Complete the postcard.

Hi Joe,
It's great here in the countryside! We're camping in a beautiful ¹ *valley*. There is a ² f _ _ _ _ _ with sheep, ³ g _ _ _ _ _ and lots of ⁴ f _ _ _ _ _ _ _ . They are really beautiful. The field has got a ⁵ f _ _ _ _ _ with a big ⁶ g _ _ _ _ . There is also a big ⁷ h _ _ _ _ and a ⁸ f _ _ _ _ _ _ with tall trees. There is a very high ⁹ m _ _ _ _ _ _ _ _ near our camp. From the top of the mountain, I can see an ¹⁰ i _ _ _ _ _ _ and the ¹¹ s _ _ _. I love it here!
Jessica

3 Look at the pictures and write the places in town.

'Where's Mum?'
'She's at the *supermarket*.'

'Where are the children?'
'They're in the _____.'

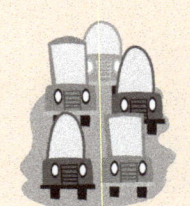

'Where's your car?'
'It's in the _____.'

'Where's Grandma?'
'She's at the _____.'

'Where are Jim and Sue?'
'They're at the _____.'

'Where are your friends?'
'They're at the _____.'

'Where are you?'
'I'm at the _____.'

'Where are you and Tony?'
'We're at the _____.'

'Where's Uncle Bob?'
'He's at the _____.'

'Where's Doctor Bell?'
'He's at the _____.'

Grammar

4 Complete the dialogues with *was, wasn't, were* or *weren't*.

- ¹ *Were* you at school yesterday?
- No, I ² _____ . I _____ at home.
- Why ³ _____ you at home?
- I ⁴ _____ sick.
- Oh, I'm sorry you ⁵ _____ well.

5 Complete the sentences with these words.

| ago evening ~~in~~ last on yesterday |

1 Julie was *in* Rome in November.
2 Max was here an hour _____ .
3 Katy wasn't at home _____ .
4 Were you at the cinema _____ night?
5 They were in the countryside _____ Sunday.
6 My friend wasn't at the party yesterday _____ .

6 Circle the correct answer.

1 Mum, (can) / *must* I go to the café with Jill, please?
2 Sally is two years old. She *can't* / *mustn't* read.
3 Students *can* / *must* always listen to their teacher.
4 You *can't* / *mustn't* walk on the flowers.
5 I *can* / *must* speak English very well.
6 Grandpa *can't* / *mustn't* run very fast. He's very old.
7 Hello. *Can* / *Must* I help you?
8 You *can't* / *mustn't* swim after your lunch.

It's dangerous.

7 Complete the sentences with the words given.

slow / slowly
1 This car is very *slow*. It is moving _____ .
amazing / amazingly
2 Stella is an _____ singer. She sings _____ .
happy / happily
3 The children are playing _____ . They're _____ .
hungry / hungrily
4 Kevin is very _____ . He's eating _____ .
quick / quickly
5 Cathy runs _____ . She's a _____ runner.
strange / strangely
6 Mr Magoo talks _____ . He's a _____ man.

My Cosmic Blog!

What can you do?

I can _____ .

I can also, _____

and I can _____ .

However, I can't _____ .

I can't _____

and I can't _____ .

Colour the stars

0-8 mistakes:
Brilliant work!

9-15 mistakes:
Great work!

More than 15 mistakes:
Good try. Revise and try again!

7a The Map

Vocabulary

1 Look at the pictures and write *True* (T) or *False* (F).

The thieves were at the zoo. **T**

The thieves carried Slinky's cage. ☐

The thieves dropped a map at the zoo. ☐

Ellie and Alex looked at the map. ☐

Alex knows the thieves are at Dark Towers. ☐

2 Circle the correct words.

catch / (drop)

zoo keeper / python

reporter / zoo keeper

catch / carry

carry / drop

strong / slim

3 Find the words and complete the opposites.

djkuglyertslimmnhbeautifuldflfatyopshortwertall

1 *ugly* ≠ b_____
2 s_____ ≠ f_____
3 t_____ ≠ s_____

4 Complete the crossword puzzle.

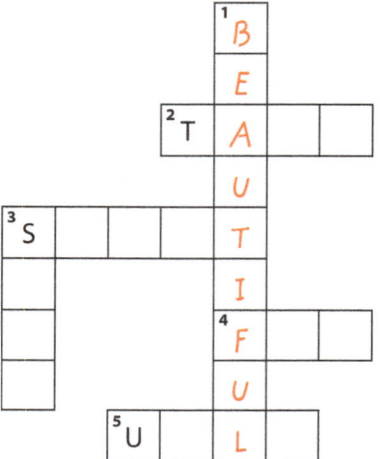

ACROSS

2

3

4

DOWN

1

3

Grammar

5 Complete the table.

Verb	Past Simple
like	1 liked
watch	2 _____
stop	3 _____
drop	4 _____
cry	5 _____
study	6 _____
play	7 _____

6 Circle the correct answers.

1 I played with my friends _____.
 a at the weekend
 b tomorrow
2 He watched a good film _____.
 a last night
 b at the moment
3 They loved their holiday in Italy _____ year.
 a next
 b last
4 My cousin studied in London two years _____.
 a before
 b ago
5 We started English _____ 2009.
 a on
 b in
6 I stayed at home on _____.
 a Thursday
 b yesterday
7 She _____ lots of books.
 a carry
 b carried
8 Tony _____ his pencil yesterday.
 a dropped
 b drops
9 We _____ hard last term.
 a studies
 b studied

7 Complete the sentences. Use the past simple of these verbs.

> carry   finish   help   listen   play   stop   taste   watch

1 The train *stopped* at the train station.
2 I _____ my homework at eight thirty.
3 Brad _____ computer games yesterday afternoon.
4 She _____ the new girl at school on Monday.
5 He _____ the football match last night.
6 We _____ our teacher's books for her.
7 Dad _____ to music at the weekend.
8 George and Carol _____ the food. It was delicious.

8 Complete the text. Use the verbs in brackets in the past simple.

Saturday 12th September

Today was a fantastic day! Dad ¹ *wanted* (want) to do something exciting. So, this morning we quickly ² _____ (finish) our breakfast. Then we ³ _____ (wash) and ⁴ _____ (clean) our teeth. After that we ⁵ _____ (cycle) to the new zoo in our town. We ⁶ _____ (follow) a path in the zoo and ⁷ _____ (look) at all the amazing animals. The zoo has got pythons. They were my favourite animals. At twelve o'clock the zoo keeper ⁸ _____ (open) the pythons' cage. Then he ⁹ _____ (carry) one round the zoo. Dad ¹⁰ _____ (love) that! Finally, the zoo keeper ¹¹ _____ (talk) to us about the animals. When we got home, my sister and I ¹² _____ (paint) beautiful pictures of our favourite animals.
Now, I'm tired, but very happy!

7b Your world

Vocabulary

1 Match.

1 I learned about
2 Jan worked
3 We studied at
4 I wanted
5 Mum filmed a
6 They were very

A with famous actors in February.
B to go on a game show last year.
C documentary last month.
D busy last term.
E animation in 2010.
F theatre school for a year.

2 Circle and write six television programmes.

```
A S B C D L Q G F S W
D O C U M E N T A R Y
Z A A O V Q Y H R A I
M P R E C C D E G N B
I O T A T U P N F Z P
X P O E C O M E D Y H
U E O N A M T W J L K
G R N G A M E S H O W
L A V R F I O J D M Q
```

1 the news
2 _____
3 _____
4 _____
5 _____
6 _____

3 Look at the pictures and write the words.

1 Mum's favourite soap opera is on every day.
2 Here's t_____ n_____ .
3 Let's watch this d_____ about animals in forests.
4 Martin studied animation last year and he made a c_____ .
5 Dad loves this g_____ s_____ because he knows all the answers.
6 'What's funny?' 'This c_____ ! It's fantastic!'

4 Complete the text with these words.

| comedy | documentary | filmed | learned |
| the news | soap operas | studied | worked |

📧 New 📧 Reply

Hi everyone! My name's Zak. I want to make a ¹ documentary about animals. What must I do?
Hi Zak! My name's Izzie. Last year, I ² _____ at the British TV and film school. I didn't make any documentaries, but I ³ _____ about film cameras. We ⁴ _____ plays, game shows and a really funny ⁵ _____ about a silly football coach! We all ⁶ _____ in a team. It was fantastic! Every year, the school does different things. This year, you can learn to make documentaries and ⁷ _____ or you can learn to read ⁸ _____ . You must go there.

Grammar

5 Circle the correct answers.
1 She _____ me last night.
   a not call
   (b) didn't call
2 _____ for help yesterday?
   a Did you ask
   b You asked
3 We didn't _____ animation in January.
   a study
   b studied
4 When _____ work at the Film and TV School?
   a you did
   b did you
5 'Did Bart watch a cartoon this morning?' 'Yes, _____.'
   a he did
   b he didn't
6 '_____ did the film finish?' 'It finished at nine o'clock.'
   a Why
   b When

6 Look at the pictures and write *True* (T) or *False* (F).

1 He didn't study for the geography test. F
2 He didn't use his mobile phone. ☐
3 She didn't wash her cat. ☐
4 She didn't clean her teeth. ☐
5 He didn't listen to music on his mp3. ☐
6 They didn't stay at home. ☐

7 Complete the sentences. Use the negative of the verbs in bold.
1 We **learned** about animation, but we *didn't learn* about documentaries.
2 They **filmed** *Mama Mia* in Greece, but they _____ *Avatar* there.
3 He **worked** in a theatre, but he _____ with famous actors.
4 I **wanted** to read the news. I _____ to be a cameraman.
5 She **studied** in London. She _____ in Paris.
6 They **liked** the comedy, but they _____ the documentary.

8 Write questions and answers. Use the past simple.
1 When / you / watch / TV (yesterday afternoon)
   When did you watch TV?
   I watched TV yesterday afternoon.
2 they / play football / yesterday (✔)
   Did they play football yesterday?
   Yes, they did.
3 What time / the lesson / start (half past ten)
   _____?
   _____.
4 Jenny / marry / an actor / last weekend (✘)
   _____?
   _____.
5 you / listen to music / last night (✘)
   _____?
   _____.
6 Jack / phone / Mary / last week (✔)
   _____?
   _____.
7 you / teeth / clean / Where / your (in the bathroom)
   _____?
   _____.
8 look at / the photo / they (✔)
   _____?
   _____.

63

7c Cosmic world

Vocabulary

1 Read the text and circle the correct answers.

✉ New ✉ Reply

My favourite television programme is *The Suite Life of Zack and Cody*. It's a comedy for children, but it isn't a cartoon. It's very funny. Zack and Cody are two brothers. They are eleven years old and they live in a hotel. Their mother works there. She works very hard. Every day, the brothers do lots of funny things. They have got two beautiful friends: Maddie and London. London's dad has got a lot of money and London is always buying new clothes. She loves fashion and always wants to be perfect. Maddie works at the hotel. She's very nice and she always helps the brothers. I watch it every afternoon!

1 *The Suite Life of Zack and Cody* is a children's _____.
  (a) comedy   b cartoon
2 _____ are eleven years old.
  a Maddie and London   b Zack and Cody
3 The brothers' mother works _____.
  a at the hotel   b in London
4 Maddie and London aren't _____.
  a beautiful   b ugly
5 London has always got _____ clothes.
  a new   b funny
6 Maddie helps _____.
  a London's dad   b Zack and Cody

2 Circle the correct words.
1 John (changed) / tried classes last month. He's now in my class and we're friends.
2 It *takes* / *changes* a long time to make a documentary.
3 The documentary was about some very *perfect* / *beautiful* insects.
4 I love this game show. It's very *funny* / *interesting*.
5 I *try* / *take* to watch my favourite TV programme twice a week.
6 This chocolate milkshake is *normal* / *perfect*.

3 Write the words.
1 ysh   shy
2 aolpr ebra _____   4 ersertpen _____
3 kyemno   _____   5 ternua   _____

4 Complete the crossword puzzle.

ACROSS
4 She has _____ long hair.
6 How long does it _____ to get to the TV studio from here?

DOWN
1 They _____ the TV programmes and now my favourite programme is on really late!
2 They filmed in the Himalayas and everything was _____.
3 I had a _____ day yesterday. Everything went wrong!
5 He _____ to film monkeys, but they took his film camera!

Grammar

5 Complete the table.

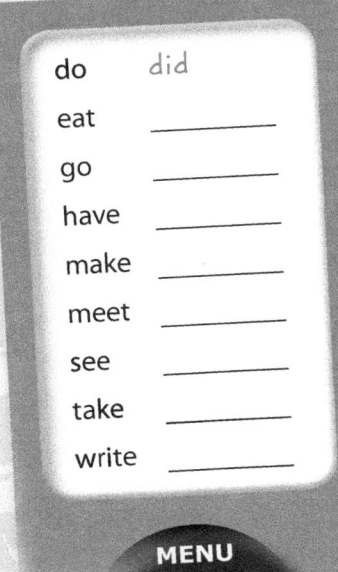

do	did
eat	_____
go	_____
have	_____
make	_____
meet	_____
see	_____
take	_____
write	_____

6 Complete the email. Use these verbs in the past simple.

> be drink do eat go make meet see

Hi Jenny,

How are you? I **¹** *went* to Italy with my class last week. **²** It _____ great! We travelled by plane and we stayed at a small, but nice hotel in Rome. We **³** _____ a lot of amazing things. For example, we visited some great museums and we **⁴** _____ a lot of old statues. My favourite place was the Colosseum. It's a fantastic place. I **⁵** _____ some new friends from Australia. We **⁶** _____ at our hotel on our first day and we **⁷** _____ pizza and **⁸** _____ delicious Italian lemonade in a café.

Lots of love,

Ann

7 Write sentences with the past simple. Use these words.

1 they / see / a snow leopard
   They saw a snow leopard.

2 he / write / to the presenter
   _____.

3 Betty / eat / lunch outside
   _____.

4 the polar bears / drink / water
   _____.

5 we / make / the documentary / in the Philippines
   _____.

6 Mum / get / new shoes / yesterday
   _____.

7 they / meet / in the Himalayan mountains
   _____.

8 The girl / drink / some juice
   _____.

8 Complete the paragraph. Use *he, him, it, them* or *they*.

My favourite television programme is *The Blue Planet*. **¹** *It* is a documentary. **²** _____ is on every Friday at seven o'clock and **³** _____ is about nature and the sea. The presenter's name is David Attenborough. **⁴** _____ is great. I really like **⁵** _____ . Last week I saw a programme about some amazing fish. **⁶** _____ were very beautiful because **⁷** _____ had a lot of different colours. A cameraman tried to swim next to **⁸** _____ . **⁹** _____ didn't look frightened but the presenter said the fish were very dangerous.

Skills 4

Reading

1 Read the text.

Lisa's birthday surprise

I had a great surprise on my birthday last week! I woke up and got out of bed quickly. It was a beautiful, sunny day. I went into the kitchen and my parents were there. They said, 'Happy birthday! We're going to London!' London? Oh, wow! It was my birthday present!

'Wait!' said my dad. 'This is for you, too.' He gave me a pretty red box. I opened it. What do you think was inside? It was a camera! 'Now, you can take photos in London,' said my mum. I was very happy!

We got in the car and drove to London. I saw beautiful fields, flowers and forests. After a few hours we arrived in London. We went to a lot of museums and I took a lot of photos. Then we went shopping. The shops in London are amazing! After a few hours, we went to a café for lunch. The food was delicious. I picked up my bag and put my hand inside. I needed my camera because I wanted to take some photos. But something was wrong. The camera wasn't in my bag! Where was it?

2 Tick (✓) what you think happened to Lisa's camera.

She left it at a museum. ☐
She lost it in the café. ☐
Someone stole it. ☐

3 Now read the end of the story. Were you right about Lisa's camera?

'When did you use it?' asked my dad. I tried to think. Was it in the clothes shop? I bought a trendy red shirt there, but I didn't use my camera. Did someone open my bag and take my camera? No, I was sure that didn't happen. And then I remembered! 'Dad, it's in the museum shop! The camera was in my hands. I bought some postcards there and I put it down.' 'Let's go back to the museum!' said my mum. We went back to the museum shop. 'I think this is yours,' said the woman in the shop, and she gave me my camera. 'I can't believe it,' I said. 'Thank you!' I had my camera again!

4 Put the story in the correct order, 1–8.
- [ ] She visited some museums.
- [ ] She bought a shirt.
- [ ] She saw the countryside.
- [1] Lisa woke up one morning.
- [ ] They returned to a museum.
- [ ] Her parents gave her a present.
- [ ] Lisa found her camera.
- [ ] They had lunch.

5 Read the texts in Exercises 1 and 3 again and answer the questions.

1 What two birthday presents did Lisa get?
   A trip to London and a camera

2 What two things did Lisa buy in London?
   _____

3 What did Lisa do in the museums?
   _____

4 Where did Lisa eat lunch in London?
   _____

5 Where did Lisa leave her camera?
   _____

Writing

6 Imagine it was your birthday last week and complete the table.

My presents:	_____
I saw:	_____
I ate:	_____
Strange or funny thing that happened:	_____
Ending:	_____

7 Use your notes from Exercise 6 to write a short story about your birthday.

My Birthday Surprise

It was my birthday last week. I was very happy. My parents gave me _____.

We went to _____.

It was fantastic! I saw _____.

For lunch, we ate _____.

But then _____!

In the end, _____.

Review 7

Vocabulary

1 Write the correct name.

Lisa

Mike

Griselda

Rufus

Maya

Nick

1. 'Who is tall?'   '*Mike* is tall.'
2. 'Who is fat?'   '_____ is fat.'
3. 'Who is short?'   '_____ is short.'
4. 'Who is ugly?'   '_____ is ugly.'
5. 'Who is slim?'   '_____ is slim.'
6. 'Who is beautiful?'   '_____ is beautiful.'

2 Complete the sentences with these words.

> ~~carry~~   catch   drop   make   marry
> read   travel   visit

1. Can you *carry* my bag to the car?
2. We always _____ to school by bus.
3. Dad didn't _____ any films last year.
4. In basketball you throw and _____ the ball.
5. Why did you _____ the glass? There's juice everywhere!
6. Pam didn't _____ Luke because she didn't love him.
7. Let's _____ Grandma this weekend.
8. I want to _____ the newspaper.

3 Complete the crossword puzzle.

```
    1Z           2G
3D  O            G
    O
    K    4C
    E    
    E         5C
6S  P
    E
    R
    
    7P
```

DOWN

1

2

4

5

ACROSS

3

6

7

68

Grammar

4 Tick (✓) the correct sentences and put a cross (✗) next to the wrong sentences.
1. I walk to school yesterday. ✗
2. Did you like the film? ☐
3. The match started five minutes ago. ☐
4. Nora didn't finishes her project yesterday. ☐
5. The girls watched a film last night. ☐
6. Did Harry studied for his history test? ☐

5 Write questions and answers. Use the past simple.

Claire / brush / her hair / last night
Did Claire brush her hair last night?
No, she didn't.

Tony / play the piano / yesterday
_____ ?
_____ .

Penny / wash her dog / at the weekend
_____ ?
_____ .

❹ Nick / play tennis / yesterday
_____ ?
_____ .

6 Complete the paragraph. Use the past simple.

Hephaestus was a Greek god. One day, Zeus ¹ *threw* (throw) him from Mount Olympus and he ² _____ (fall) on the island of Lemnos. After that, Hephaestus ³ _____ (not walk) very well because he ⁴ _____ (have) a problem with his foot. The other gods ⁵ _____ (laugh) at him and he ⁶ _____ (feel) bad. But he ⁷ _____ (make) beautiful things with gold and silver and people ⁸ _____ (like) them.

7 Complete the blog.

My Cosmic Blog! ✗

Tell us about your favourite hero from the past.
What did he or she do?

My favourite hero is _____.
_____ was amazing because
_____.
_____. Also,
_____. That's why
_____ was great!

Colour the Stars

0-8 mistakes:
Brilliant work!

9-15 mistakes:
Great work!

More than 15 mistakes:
Good try. Revise and try again!

8a Dark Towers

Vocabulary

1 Match the pictures to the sentences.

A The woman is taller than the man. But the man is stronger.
B Whose is this key?
C We're looking for a place called 'Dark Towers'.
D Thank you for your help. We must go now.

2 Circle the correct words.

1 smile / kick

4 high / rude

2 high / rich

5 kick / rude

3 nose / noise

6 rude / rich

3 Look at the pictures and write the face and body words.

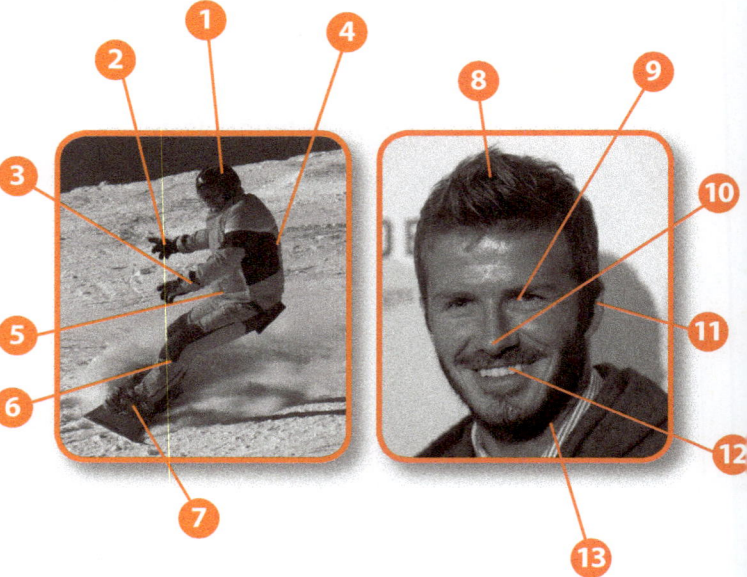

1 d e h a	head	8 r i h a	_____
2 d a n h	_____	9 y e e	_____
3 r m a	_____	10 o s e n	_____
4 c a k b	_____	11 a r e	_____
5 m t y u m	_____	12 u t o h m	_____
6 e g l	_____	13 c e k n	_____
7 t o f o	_____		

4 Complete the sentences with these words.

> eye   hair   hand   ~~high~~   leg   noise
> rich   rude

1 Don't climb the wall. It's really *high*.
2 'Why are you walking like that?' 'My _____ hurts.'
3 Those people never talk to anyone. They're very _____.
4 Have a shower and wash your _____ after swimming in the pool.
5 Take my _____ and let's cross the road.
6 'What's that horrible _____?' 'Oh, my brother is playing piano!'
7 My uncle is very _____ and lives in a very big house.
8 I can't see because I can't open my left _____!

Grammar

5 Complete the table.

Adjective	Comparative
big	1 bigger
tall	2 _____
naughty	3 _____
rude	4 _____
expensive	5 _____
famous	6 _____
good	7 _____
bad	8 _____

6 Circle the correct words.
1. Australia is *hotter / more hot* than England.
2. Your mobile phone is *nicer than / nicer* mine.
3. Singers are usually *more famous / famous* than dancers.
4. This TV programme looks *good / better* than that one.
5. I'm *taller / more taller* than my mum.
6. Kittens are *funny / funnier* than cats.

7 Read the email and write the adjectives in the comparative.

Hi Sharon,
How are you? I'm fine.
I met your sister yesterday. She's very nice. Is she ¹ _____ (tall) than you? Aren't you twins? You don't look like twins. You are ² _____ (slim) than her and ³ _____ (pretty)!
I got a new computer game today. It was ⁴ _____ (expensive) than my old one. But it's ⁵ _____ (good). Come and play it at the weekend. Mum can make us strawberry smoothies. Her smoothies are ⁶ _____ (delicious) than mine.
Bye for now,
Jill

8 Complete the sentences. Use comparative adjectives and *than*.

~~cold~~   expensive   fast   good   high   noisy

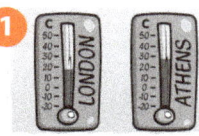 London's *colder than* Athens.

 Motorbikes are _____ cars.

 The baby is _____ the children.

 Water is _____ lemonade for your teeth.

 Mountains are _____ than hills.

 The digital camera's _____ the mp3 player.

9 Write sentences with these words. Use comparatives and *than*.
1. pigs / be / fat / chickens
   Pigs are fatter than chickens.
2. snakes / be / dangerous / parrots
   _____.
3. a polar bear / be / strong / a monkey
   _____.
4. be / Tom / naughty / Jerry
   _____?
5. be / your mum / slim / mine
   _____?
6. I / be / good at / Maths / History
   _____.
7. Our new teacher / be / nice / our old one
   _____.
8. Beyoncé / be / famous / Adele.
   _____.

71

8b Your world

Vocabulary

1 Tick (✔) the correct pictures.

1 Which animal is the heaviest?

A ✔   B ☐   C ☐

2 Which animal has got the most legs?

A ☐   B ☐   C ☐

3 Which animal has got the longest ears?

A ☐   B ☐   C ☐

4 Which animal has got the longest tail?

A ☐   B ☐   C ☐

5 Which animal is the widest?

A ☐   B ☐   C ☐

2 Circle and write eight animal words.

```
S W G I R A F F E G
H C F T W O R P A O
A A O H B W S L S R
R M X A N L F S U I
K E A L O C A M E L
T C H E E T A H R L
E L E P H A N T T A
```

1 giraffe
2 _____
3 _____
4 _____
5 _____
6 _____
7 _____
8 _____

3 Read the clues and write the animals.

What am I?

1 I am the fastest cat. I'm a c h e e t a h.
2 I travel in the desert. I'm a c _ _ _ _ _.
3 I have got the longest nose. I'm an e _ _ _ _ _ _ _ _.
4 I look like a monkey, but I'm bigger and heavier. I'm a g _ _ _ _ _ _ _.
5 I'm very dangerous and I live in the sea. I'm a s _ _ _ _ _.
6 I'm the cleverest bird. I'm an o _ _.
7 I'm the tallest animal and I've got the longest neck. I'm a g _ _ _ _ _ _ _.
8 I live in the forest and I've got a big tail. I'm a f _ _.

Grammar

4 Complete the table.

Adjective	Superlative
tall	1 *the tallest*
rude	2 _____
fat	3 _____
naughty	4 _____
expensive	5 _____
bad	6 _____
good	7 _____

5 Circle the correct answers.
1. Are sharks _____ animals in the sea?
   a most dangerous
   b the most dangerous
2. Swiper is _____ fox on TV.
   a the most famous
   b the more famous
3. My kitten is _____ of all my pets.
   a the naughty
   b the naughtiest
4. Jack is _____ boy in the class.
   a bigger
   b the biggest
5. Which is _____ mountain in the world?
   a the high
   b the highest
6. This zoo is _____ in the country.
   a the best
   b the good
7. Which horse is _____ of the three?
   a the quieter
   b the quietest
8. He's _____ unfriendly person in the neighbourhood.
   a the most
   b more

6 Complete the text with the words in brackets. Use the superlative.

Hi, I'm Jo. I love animals and my favourite cartoon is *Dora the Explorer*. She is ¹ *the most famous* (famous) little girl on TV. Dora has got a friend called Boots. He is a monkey, but he is Dora's best friend. There are many animals in the cartoon. Boots is ² _____ (nice) animal. He helps Dora find things and they take animals to their homes. Dora and Boots can climb ³ _____ (high) mountains and ⁴ _____ (tall) trees. They can also cross ⁵ _____ (dangerous) rivers. There is also a fox called Swiper. He is ⁶ _____ (naughty) animal in the cartoon. Swiper's always trying to steal things, but Dora and Boots usually stop him. I love *Dora the Explorer* because it's ⁷ _____ (good) cartoon ever!

7 Write questions and answer for you. Use the superlative.
1. Who / be / funny / person you know
   Who is the funniest person you know?
   student's own answer.
2. Who / be / young / person / in your class
   _____ ?
   _____ .
3. Which / comic / be / good / for you
   _____ ?
   _____ .
4. Which / animal / be / noisy
   _____ ?
   _____ .
5. Which / food / be / bad / for you
   _____ ?
   _____ .
6. Who / be / tall / in your family
   _____ ?
   _____ .
7. What / be / expensive / toy / you've got
   _____ ?
   _____ .

8c Cosmic world

Vocabulary

1 Label the monsters with these words.

dragon   King Kong   ~~Shrek~~   the Cyclops

1 Shrek

2 _____

3 _____

4 _____

2 Match.

1

2

3

4

5

6

A forehead

B scary

C fight

D get married

E building

F friendly

3 Complete the crossword puzzle.

```
          ¹G
   ²F     E
          T
          M
      ³S  A
          R
          R
       ⁴F I
         E
   ⁵B     D
```

ACROSS

2 There's a mosquito on your _____!
3 Cerberus was a very _____ dog with three heads.
4 You mustn't _____ in the playground.
5 The tallest _____ in the world is in Dubai.

DOWN

1 They want to _____ on an island.
2 Mr Jones is the _____ teacher in the school.

Grammar

4 Circle the correct words.
1. I'm (better) / the best at Maths than History.
2. The whale is the heaviest / heavier animal of all.
3. Ogres are scarier / the scariest than dragons.
4. Mermaids are the most beautiful / more beautiful than dragons.
5. Harry's the worst / worse player in the team.
6. Gorillas aren't bigger / biggest than whales.
7. Which is the most expensive / more expensive car in the world?

5 Complete the email. Use comparative and superlative adjectives.

Hi Rob,

How are you? I went to the cinema last weekend. I saw a film called *Avatar*. It was **1** *the best* (good) film of the year for me. In the film, the Na'vi tribe live in a place called Pandora. They are trying to save their trees and nature. They are **2** _____ (friendly) than the people. They are also **3** _____ (big) than the Earth people. There is a really horrible man called Colonel Quaritch. He is **4** _____ (bad) person of all. He starts a big fight in the middle of **5** _____ (beautiful) forest in Pandora. The Na'vi are **6** _____ (strong) than the horrible people and they win.

Write to me with your news.

Bye for now,

Jamie

6 Correct the sentences.
1. He play in the garden in the evening. *plays*
2. A spider have got eight legs. _____
3. It never snow in July in France. _____
4. The Cyclops is ugly than Shrek. _____
5. I likes friendly monsters. _____
6. Giants are heavier from people. _____
7. She is the more beautiful girl in the world. _____
8. They watches Shrek often. _____
9. Do you knows the Hydra? _____
10. Cerberus is scariest dog. _____

7 Write questions and answers for you. Use the comparative and the superlative.
1. be / your mum / young / your dad
   Is your mum younger than your dad?
   student's own answer.
2. What's / beautiful / place in your country
   _____?
   _____.
3. be / dragons / nice / ogres
   _____?
   _____.
4. What / food / be / good for you
   _____?
   _____.
5. Which / monster / be / funny
   _____?
   _____.
6. be / England / hot / your country
   _____?
   _____.

Review 8

Vocabulary

1 Write True (T) or False (F).

1 camel
   a It's a tall animal. **T**
   b You can ride on its back. **T**
   c It lives in a tree. **F**
2 cheetah
   a It's the fastest animal.
   b It hasn't got a tail.
   c It's a big cat.
3 elephant
   a It's got a small tummy.
   b It's very heavy.
   c It's got big ears.
4 fox
   a It's got four legs.
   b It's got a short tail.
   c It looks like a dog.
5 giraffe
   a It's got a long neck.
   b It lives in Africa.
   c It's got wings.
6 gorilla
   a It's got a big head.
   b It isn't heavy.
   c It's got hands.
7 owl
   a It sleeps at night.
   b It's a bird.
   c It's got big eyes.
8 shark
   a It lives in the sea.
   b It's dangerous.
   c It's got long ears.

2 Circle the odd word out.

1 bad   (good)   naughty
2 short   tall   high
3 slow   fast   quick
4 friendly   dangerous   nice
5 rude   unfriendly   nice

3 Write the body words.

1 *arm*   rma
2 _____   ackb
3 _____   aer
4 _____   eesy
5 _____   otof
6 _____   rhai
7 _____   ndha
8 _____   dahe
9 _____   gle
10 _____   umtoh

76

Grammar

4 Choose the correct answers.

1 Your car is _____ my car.
 a nice than
 (b) nicer than
2 Lucy is very _____ !
 a naughty
 b naughtier
3 The new café is worse _____ the old café!
 a from
 b than
4 Mount Everest is _____ than Mount Olympus.
 a higher
 b high
5 This book is _____ than that one.
 a better
 b more good

5 Complete the sentences with comparative adjectives and *than*.

1 Scarlet is *taller than* (tall) Sid.
2 Sid is _____ (fat) Scarlet.
3 Scarlet's hair is _____ (long) Sid's.
4 Sid's legs are _____ (short) Scarlet's.
5 Sid isn't _____ (slim) Scarlet.
6 Sid is _____ (ugly) Scarlet.
7 Scarlet's clothes are _____ (nice) Sid's.
8 Scarlet's shoes are _____ (high) Sid's.

6 Complete the paragraph with superlative adjectives.

Do you know Koko? She is ¹ *the most famous* (famous) gorilla in the world because she is ² _____ (clever). Koko can 'say' more than 1,000 words with her hands, and she understands more than 2,000 words in English. When she is hungry, she puts her hand on her tummy. Koko's teacher says she is ³ _____ (good) student. She is also ⁴ _____ (nice) friend – she plays with little kittens. Koko is ⁵ _____ (amazing) animal!

7 Complete the blog

My Cosmic Blog!

Tell us about your favourite animal.
What does it look like?
Why is it special?

My favourite animal is the _____.

It's got _____.

It has also got _____.

It's special because._____.

It's also, _____.

Colour the Stars

0-8 mistakes:
Brilliant work!

9-15 mistakes:
Great work!

More than 15 mistakes:
Good try. Revise and try again!

Vocabulary

1 Match the pictures to the sentences.

A Sid, come here. I've got a problem with some kids.

B Fly away, Echo. Quick!

C Take this key. We're going to ring the doorbell.

D That parrot is going to stay here with me.

E Read the words on my T-shirt, horrible children!

2 Complete the phrases with these words.

> be (x2)   excuse   go   teach   wait

1 *Go* away!
2 _____ a minute!
3 _____ careful!
4 _____ me, Miss.
5 I'll _____ them a lesson.
6 You'll _____ sorry!

3 Circle the odd one out.

1 tracksuit   trainers   scarf
2 dress   jacket   skirt
3 hat   trousers   jeans
4 shoes   socks   sweater
5 t-shirt   boots   top

4 Complete the clothes words.

1 j e a n s
2 s _ _ _ _ _
3 s _ _ _ _ _
4 j _ _ _ _ _ _
5 s _ _ _ _ _ _ _
6 d _ _ _ _ _
7 s _ _ _ _ _
8 t _ _ _ _ _ _ _ _
9 s _ _ _ _ _
10 b _ _ _ _ _

Grammar

5 Match the questions and answers.
1. What are you going to buy?
2. Where are they going to walk to?
3. Are you going to go to Tim's birthday party, Frank?
4. Is Judy going to wear her tracksuit and trainers for PE?
5. Are they going to have a picnic tomorrow?
6. Are you and Manos going to play tennis today?
7. Is David going to get a new computer game?

A No, they aren't.
B Yes, I am.
C Yes, he is.
D They're going to walk to the supermarket.
E I'm going to buy a hat.
F No, we aren't.
G Yes, she is.

6 Circle the correct words.
1. *I'm* / I going to Japan this summer.
2. What are you *go* / *going* to get Sam for his birthday on Saturday?
3. Look at those black clouds. It *is going to rain* / *going to rain*.
4. He *isn't going* / *not going* to play for the school football team this year.
5. I'm not going *to wear* / *wearing* that hat! It looks silly.
6. Their dog is dangerous. What are they going to *doing* / *do* with it?
7. We are *going to have* / *go to having* a great time at the zoo.

7 Complete the sentences with the verbs in brackets. Use *going to*.
1. Hurry up. We *are going to be* (be) late.
2. He _____ (not do) any homework.
3. It _____ (be) really hot this weekend. Let's go to the beach.
4. My football team is the best. They _____ (win) the game.
5. I want some new jeans. I _____ (go) shopping.
6. _____ (you see) the new film?
7. _____ (she get) an mp3 player?

8 Write questions and short answers. Use *going to*.

1. the girl with the dress / smile   (✘)
   Is the girl with the dress going to smile? No, she isn't.
2. the boy with the jeans and trainers / take a photo   (✔)
   _____?
   _____.
3. the girl with the skirt and jacket / fall   (✘)
   _____?
   _____.
4. the boy with the hat / do PE later   (✔)
   _____?
   _____.
5. the boy with the sweater and trousers / eat spaghetti   (✘)
   _____?
   _____.
6. the four children / dance   (✘)
   _____?
   _____.

9b Your world

Vocabulary

1 Circle the words and complete the sentences.

mn clean rtyjourneyopicookasdrobotnmkspaceshipmlroof

1 My bike is dirty. I'm going to *clean* it.
2 I want to go on a _____ around the world.
3 What an amazing _____! It can do all my homework.
4 One day we'll travel to Mars in a _____.
5 Let's _____ dinner for Mum and Dad tonight.
6 Look at that cat! It's up on the _____.

2 Match.

A summer
B winter
C autumn
D spring

3 Look at the pictures and write *True* (T) or *False* (F).

1 It's sunny.   F   4 It's windy.   ☐
2 It's stormy.   ☐   5 It's snowing. ☐
3 It's raining. ☐   6 It's cloudy. ☐

4 Complete the text with these words.

> it's cloudy   it's raining   it's snowing
> it's sunny   it's windy   ~~summer~~   winter

Here's today's weather. It's July 25th and it's a very hot ¹ *summer* here in Athens. This morning, ² _____ in all of the city. On the Greek islands, it's hot but ³ _____ and some boats cannot leave. In Thessaloniki the weather is worse than in Athens. In some parts of the city ⁴ _____ and in other parts ⁵ _____. But don't worry because the weather is going to be much better in Thessaloniki tomorrow. At least it isn't ⁶ _____ like it is in Australia. In Sydney ⁷ _____ this morning!

5 Complete for you.

📧 New   ↩ Reply

My favourite season is _____ because it's
_____.

80

Grammar

6 Choose the correct answers.

1 People _____ use small spaceships in the future.
   a will ⓐ
   b will be
2 Rich people _____ on holiday to Mars in 2090.
   a will go
   b are
3 Children won't _____ to school.
   a not go
   b go
4 It _____ hotter in the future.
   a is being
   b will be
5 People _____ cook food.
   a they not
   b won't
6 There will _____ swimming pools and gardens on roofs.
   a be
   b being

7 Match.

1 Will I go swimming this summer?
2 Will he go on a journey in a spaceship?
3 Will the weather be colder in 2090?
4 Will robots clean houses in the future?
5 Will we go to school in 2090?
6 Will you be happy in the future, Rob?

A Yes, they will.
B Yes, I will.
C No, we won't.
D Yes, you will.
E No, he won't.
F No, it won't.

8 Look at the weather in London for next week and correct the sentences.

	London
Monday	🌧️
Wednesday	🌬️
Friday	❄️
Sunday	☀️

1 It will snow in London on Monday.
   It won't snow in London on Monday. It will rain.
2 It will be sunny in London on Wednesday.
   _____
3 It will be windy in London on Friday.
   _____
4 It will rain in London on Sunday.
   _____

9 Write questions and answers. Use *will* or *won't*.

1 computers / teach / children (✔)
   Will computers teach children?
   Yes, they will.
2 people / have / robot pets (✔)
   _____?
   _____.
3 children / like / school in the future (✘)
   _____?
   _____.
4 the weather / always be / sunny in the future (✘)
   _____?
   _____.
5 you / go on / an amazing journey / in the summer (✔)
   _____?
   _____.
6 your teacher / give you / a test / on Monday (✘)
   _____?
   _____.

9C Cosmic world

Vocabulary

1 Look at the pictures and write *True* (T) or *False* (F).

1 Ross is wearing a kilt. **T**
2 Atsuko is wearing nice black trainers. ☐
3 Ed is wearing a horrible striped tie. ☐
4 Jane is wearing a boring white shirt. ☐
5 Ross is wearing long white socks. ☐
6 Keiko has got a nice new bag. ☐

2 Circle and write the six fashion words.

B	A	C	K	P	A	C	K
L	S	N	P	N	M	T	G
E	T	H	S	N	Q	C	N
B	R	A	C	E	L	E	T
T	I	I	M	C	D	O	I
I	P	R	X	A	L	I	E
N	E	C	K	L	A	C	E
C	D	L	E	N	B	X	S
R	U	I	L	P	V	Y	I
T	B	P	D	E	R	Q	U

1 *tie* 4 _____
2 _____ 5 _____
3 _____ 6 _____

3 Complete the sentences.

1 I really like your new *backpack*.

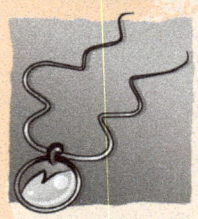
2 Mum's buying me a new _____.

3 Have you got a yellow _____?

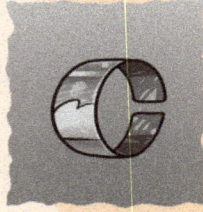
4 Wow! That's a lovely _____!

5 I've got a new _____ shirt.

6 Dad always wears a red _____ to work.

4 Complete the word groups.

> backpack   kilt   necklace   tie   socks   T-shirt

1 bag, sporran, *backpack*
2 boots, shoes, _____
3 bracelet, hair clip, _____
4 school uniform, trousers, _____
5 top, sweater, _____
6 skirt, dress, _____

Grammar

5 Circle the correct words.
1. I'm wearing my (old blue) / blue old jeans.
2. That's a *black beautiful / beautiful black* jacket.
3. She's wearing a *dirty grey / grey dirty* skirt.
4. Are you going to buy that *purple big / big purple* backpack?
5. Can you give me your *new brown / brown new* shoes?
6. Here are some *nice red / red nice* hairclips for you.

6 Tick (✔) the correct sentences and correct the wrong ones.
1. He's buying a horrible orange tie. ✔
2. My favourite clothes are my pink new dress and my white jacket.
   new pink
3. In winter, Mum wears expensive grey boots.
   _____
4. I must wash my blue dirty tracksuit.
   _____
5. There aren't any nice yellow necklaces in the shop.
   _____
6. It's cold outside. Put on your red warm sweater.
   _____
7. She's wearing her black beautiful jacket.
   _____
8. I haven't got a white clean shirt.
   _____

7 Describe the people's clothes. Use these words.

jacket / clean / white
She's wearing a clean white jacket.

trainers / black / new
_____.

school tie / horrible / black
_____.

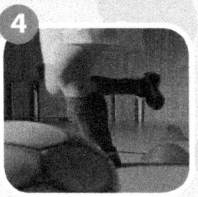

socks / red / long
_____.

top / funny / brown
_____.

hat / cool / white
_____.

8 Correct the punctuation.

Hi, everyone. I'm p̂atsy. I'm from America. i really love clothes and fashion! At the moment, I'm wearing a new pink dress. It's fantastic? My favourite things are my red scarf my purple shoes and my green jacket. I love colours! My mum says, Patsy don't wear so many colours! but I don't listen to her What about you. Do you love colours too?

Reading

1 Read the emails. Find and correct the ten mistakes.

✉ New ↩ Reply

To: Andy
From: Jim
Subject: Weather

Hi andy,

How are you? Did you finish your exams. I hope you get good marks!

I finished school yesterday and my sumer holidays started today. Im really excited. It's hot and sunny today and I'm going to go swimming in the afternoon with my friends. The beach is near my house and I only needs to take my swimsuit with me. I can walk there in two minutes. I've got six weeks of summer holidays. Are your summer holidays longer or shorter than mine?

It will be Christmas soon. Does that sound strange to you? I know it's winter in England for you, but it's summer for me here in Australia! Is it very cold there now? Australia is hotter than England. We're luckier than you

Bye for now,

Jim

✉ New ↩ Reply

To: Jim
From: Andy
Subject: Christmas

Hi Jim,

It was great to get your email. I'm very well, thanks. I finished my exams and I got good marks, but some marks were better than others. Oh well, I must try harder next term.

My christmas holidays started today, too, but I'm going stay home because the weather is bad. You're so lucky! It's winter here and it's cloudy and windy today. Tomorrow it's going to be stormy! I won't spend my holidays on the beach! Christmas in summer seem very strange to me. But it's great for you! I must wear heavy winter clothes like boots a scarf, a sweater and a jacket, but you can wear your swimsuit. I want to live in Australia! The weather is better! And the summer holidays are longer – I only gets five weeks in the summer!

Have a Merry Christmas!

Andy

2 Read the emails again and complete the sentences with *Jim* or *Andy*.

1 *Jim* lives in Australia.
2 _____ got good marks at school.
3 Today, _____ will go to the beach.
4 Today, _____ will stay at home.
5 _____ must wear a sweater.
6 _____ isn't going to wear boots.

3 Write the comparative adjectives and *than*.

1 The summer holidays in Australia are *longer than* (long) in England.
2 England is _____ (cold) Australia.
3 Jim is _____ (lucky) Andy.
4 The weather in England isn't _____ (good) the weather in Australia.
5 Andy's clothes are _____ (heavy) Jim's clothes.
6 Christmas in Australia is _____ (hot) in England.

Writing

4 Read the emails again and circle the correct words for your country.

1 In my country, we have Christmas in *summer / winter*.
2 We have *longer / shorter* summer holidays than in Australia.
3 In my country, the weather is *better than / worse than* in England.
4 England is *cloudier than / sunnier than* my country.

5 Complete the sentences about the weather in your country.

In _____ (your country) in summer, the weather is _____ (describe the weather).
In summer, I wear _____ (say what clothes you wear).
In summer, I _____ (say what activities you do).
We get _____ weeks summer holidays.

In winter, the weather is _____ (describe the weather).
In winter, I wear _____ (say what clothes you wear).
In winter, I _____ (say what activities you do).

6 Write an email to Jim in Australia or Andy in England. Tell him about your country and compare it to his. Use your answers from Exercise 5.

✉ New ✉ Reply

Hi _____,
How are you?
Let me tell you about my summer holidays. We get _____ weeks. That's _____ yours. Also, in the summer, it's _____, so I wear _____ and I go to _____. Summer here is _____ than summer in _____.
Winter and summer are very different here. In winter, the weather is _____, and I must wear _____. I can't go _____ because the weather is _____.
I think winter here is _____ than the winter in _____.
Bye for now,

_____
(your name)

Review 9

Vocabulary

1 Where do you wear these clothes? Put them in the correct group.

> boots hat jacket jeans scarf shirt
> shoes skirt socks sweater top
> trainers trousers T-shirt

1	hat	8	boots
2	___	9	___
3	___	10	___
4	___	11	___
5	___	12	___
6	___	13	___
7	___	14	___

2 Match.

1 It's raining.
2 It's sunny.
3 It's windy.
4 It's stormy.
5 It's snowing.
6 It's cloudy.

A Oh, no! I lost my hat.
B What a lot of noise!
C I can't see the sky.
D Have you got an umbrella?
E Everything outside is white.
F Let's go to the beach.

3 Write the seasons.

In Europe, it's ¹ winter from December to February. Then, from March to May it's ² _____. After that comes ³ _____ from June to August. Then it's ⁴ _____ from September to November. In Australia, Argentina and South Africa, it's all different! Students have their summer holidays in December!

4 Write the words.

School uniform

In Britain, students wear a school uniform. The girls wear a ¹ skirt or a ² d _ _ _ _ _, and the boys wear ³ t _ _ _ _ _ _ _. They both wear a ⁴ s _ _ _ _ and a ⁵ j _ _ _ _ _. At some schools, the students wear a ⁶ h _ _ and a ⁷ t _ _. In winter, they wear a ⁸ s _ _ _ _ _ _. For PE, students can wear a ⁹ T-_ _ _ _ _ _, shorts or a ¹⁰ t _ _ _ _ _ _ _ _.

Grammar

5 Write sentences with *going to*.

1 Harry / buy / that blue sweater
   Is Harry going to buy that blue sweater?
2 my cousin / be / a doctor
   _____.
3 I / not have / dinner
   _____.
4 the boys / play / football
   _____?
5 Anita / not wear / her boots
   _____.
6 Mum / wash / my red T-shirt
   _____.

6 Complete the sentences with the adjectives.

1 *Do you like my new red mobile phone?* (red, new)

2 Joe is wearing _____ socks. (white, old)

3 I've got a _____ jacket. (beautiful, green)

4 Hector's got a _____ puppy. (cute, black)

5 I want a _____ bike. (blue, fast)

6 Tina is buying a _____ skirt. (yellow, long)

7 Correct the mistakes.

1 Will we lives on other planets?   live
2 It will be not cloudy tomorrow.   _____
3 Will have we robots for pets?   _____
4 People will travelling in space.   _____
5 Will computers doing everything for us?   _____
6 Cars will to fly.   _____

8 Complete the blog.

My Cosmic Blog! ✕

Tell us your predictions for the future.

In the future, I think _____ will
_____.

Also, _____
_____.

We won't _____.

And we won't _____.

Colour the Stars

0-8 mistakes:
Brilliant work!

9-15 mistakes:
Great work!

More than 15 mistakes:
Good try. Revise and try again!

10a We got them!

Vocabulary

1 Match the sentences to the pictures.

> Fantastic! It's the right key.
> We've got Scarlet and Sid!
> ~~Echo wants to tell us something.~~
> Wow! We're famous.

1. Echo wants to tell us something.

2. _____

3. _____

4. _____

2 Circle the correct words.

1. Who's (paying) / selling for the tickets?
2. Look! There's a photo of Gran in this *newspaper* / *rest*.
3. Why did Lucy *pay* / *sell* her mp3 player?
4. Let's sit here because I need a *torch* / *rest*.
5. It's dark outside. Don't forget your *torch* / *newspaper*.

3 Find and write the thirteen holiday words.

```
S S L E E P I N G B A G
P W E V Q A T C T S T S
A I U M B R E L L A E H
S M M S U I O N L N N E
S S U I T C A S E D T L
P U R C A M P S I T E L
O I P O S T C A R D C S
R T I C K E T S C A P K
T H O R S E R I D I N G
```

1 *umbrella*   8 _____
2 _____   9 _____
3 _____   10 _____
4 _____   11 _____
5 _____   12 _____
6 _____   13 _____
7 _____

4 Complete the text.

Hi Alex and Ellie,
How are you? I saw your picture in yesterday's ¹ *newspaper* 🗞️. You two are brilliant! I'm on holiday with my family at the moment. We're staying in a campsite. I love sleeping in a ² _____ ⛺. I've got a really nice blue ³ _____ 🔦. It's very dark at night here, but luckily we've got a big ⁴ _____ 🔦. I'm writing this ⁵ _____ 📇 in a quiet café on the beach. It's a really beautiful beach and we can swim all day. In the evenings, I walk along the beach and collect ⁶ _____ 🐚. I've got more than one hundred! Tomorrow, we're all going ⁷ _____ 🐴. It'll be great fun.
Have fun in Scotland!
Love,
Don

Grammar

5 Circle the correct words. Then write *Present* (P) or *Future* (F).
1 *I'm* / I getting a new swimsuit this afternoon. **F**
2 What are you *doing / do* this weekend? ☐
3 Look, *it rains / it's raining* and I haven't got my umbrella. ☐
4 Jamie *isn't coming / doesn't come* to the beach with us tomorrow. ☐
5 Where *is / are* you going on holiday this summer? ☐
6 Who *is eating / eats* that delicious ice cream? ☐
7 Hi Mum, *I'm calling / I call* from London. ☐
8 They are *have / having* a great time at the campsite. ☐

6 Complete the dialogue with the verbs in brackets. Use the present continuous.

Stella: Hi Rob, it's Stella. What ¹ *are you doing* (do)?
Rob: Oh, Stella hi. I'm with John and Cathy. We ² _____ (lie) on the beach. How about you?
Stella: I'm bored. I ³ _____ (not go) out today because my parents ⁴ _____ (not feel) well.
Rob: Oh, that's too bad. Hey, we ⁵ _____ (go) to the cinema near you later. Come with us.
Stella: Thanks Rob, that sounds great! What film ⁶ _____ (play)?
Rob: It's a new comedy with Ben Stiller.
Stella: What time ⁷ _____ (you go)?
Rob: We ⁸ _____ (meet) at the cinema at seven o'clock. See you then, OK?
Stella: Brilliant! See you then, Rob. Bye bye.

7 Look at Bob's diary. Write sentences about his plans for the week.

Monday
buy a tent
Tuesday
take Mum for lunch
Wednesday
wash my sleeping bag
Thursday
get the plane tickets
Friday
put my clothes in my suitcase
Saturday
fly to Mykonos
Sunday
read the newspaper on the beach

1 *On Monday, Bob's buying a tent.*
2 _____.
3 _____.
4 _____.
5 _____.
6 _____.
7 _____.

8 Answer the questions about you.
1 Where are you going this weekend?
   Student's own answer.
2 What time are you having lunch tomorrow?
   _____.
3 How are you travelling to school next week?
   _____.
4 When are you going on holiday this summer?
   _____.
5 Who are you playing with this evening?
   _____.
6 Which clothes are you wearing to school tomorrow?
   _____.

10b Your world

Vocabulary

1 Complete the sentences with these words.

> crossing ~~ice~~ peaceful roads
> tiny tourists

1 You drive a snowmobile on *ice* .
2 Our town is quite big, but it's _____ in winter.
3 How long does the _____ from England to France take by boat?
4 Lots of _____ visit the museum every day.
5 This _____ house has only got two rooms.
6 In Athens, the _____ are very busy and dangerous.

2 Look at the pictures and complete the sentences.

1 We're travelling from France to Italy by *coach*.

2 Have you got your tickets for the _____?

3 The _____ is flying over the island.

4 We have to show our passports before we get on the _____ .

5 My brother is going to get a _____ .

6 This _____ is carrying a lot of things.

7 There are a lot of tourists from America on the _____ .

8 This _____ travels through fields and mountains.

3 Write Land, Sea or Air.

1 ferry — *Sea*
2 coach — _____
3 ship — _____
4 plane — _____
5 train — _____
6 motorbike — _____
7 lorry — _____
8 helicopter — _____

4 Complete the crossword puzzle.

```
        ¹R    ²C
   ³T    O                    ⁴M
        A
        D
                  ⁵C
   ⁶H
                              ⁷I
```

ACROSS
3 Many _____ go to hot countries in summer.
6 I love planes, but I don't like travelling by _____ .
7 Careful! There's _____ on the garden path.

DOWN
1 Always look left and right when you cross the *road*.
2 The ferry _____ only took an hour.
4 A _____ can travel faster than a car.
5 We travelled by _____ from the airport to our hotel.

Grammar

5 Match the questions and answers.

1 Do I have to bring sandwiches and a drink?
2 Does he have to wear a hat on the beach?
3 Do you have to get up early on Saturdays, Josh?
4 What do we have to wear on the trip?
5 Does she have to bring a towel?
6 Do they have to pay for the trip this week?
7 When do they have to be on the coach?

A Yes, she does.
B You have to wear your school uniform.
C Yes, you do.
D They have to be there at eight o'clock.
E No, I don't.
F No, they don't.
G Yes, he does.

6 Choose the correct answers.

1 We _____ to be at the train station at two o'clock.
 a has
 b have
2 They _____ to come by ferry.
 a not have
 b don't have
3 'Do I have to go on the trip?' 'Yes, _____.'
 a you do
 b I do
4 She has _____ a tracksuit.
 a to bring
 b bring
5 _____ show his passport?
 a Has he to
 b Does he have to
6 'Does the lorry have to stop here?' 'No, it _____.'
 a doesn't
 b isn't

7 Write the opposite of these sentences.

1 He has to get up early tomorrow.
 He doesn't have to get up early tomorrow.
2 I don't have to go to the dentist next week.
 _____.
3 She has to clean her room.
 _____.
4 We don't have to get a new tent.
 _____.
5 You have to take a torch.
 _____.
6 They don't have to visit Lulworth Cove.
 _____.

8 Write the words in the correct order.

1 grandparents' / his / at / has / stay / He / this weekend / to
 He has to stay at his grandparents' this weekend.
2 to / any / don't / bring / You / have / towels
 _____.
3 year / laptop / have / get / I / a / to / next
 _____.
4 have / your tickets / pay / today / You / for / to
 _____.
5 does / go / to / Dad / Why / have / America / to
 _____?
6 glasses / has / Who / buy / to
 _____?
7 wear / have / Nancy / today / doesn't / a / to / uniform
 _____.
8 has / My brother / to / motorbike / clean / his
 _____.

91

10c Cosmic world

Vocabulary

1 Write the places beside each photo.

> A boat trip on the Thames   Camden Market
> Hyde Park   The London Eye
> The Tower of London

 A boat trip on the Thames

 _____

 _____

 _____

 _____

2 Choose the correct answers.

How well do you know London?
Do this quick quiz to find out!

1 _____ is a famous clock in London.
  a Big Ben   b The London Eye
2 _____ is one of the biggest toy shops in the world.
  a Camden Market   b Hamley's
3 You can see dinosaurs at the _____.
  a Natural History Museum   b Tower of London
4 You can go on a boat trip on the River _____ in London.
  a Thames   b Hyde
5 The _____ is a very old castle.
  a Big Ben   b Tower of London

3 Match.

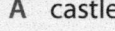

A castle
B pancakes
C fish and chips
D dinosaur
E one thousand

4 Complete the sentences with these words.

> castle   dinosaur   fish and chips
> one thousand   pancakes

1 I want to stay in a *castle* in Scotland.
2 My favourite breakfast is _____ with butter and sugar.
3 _____ tourists visited the London Eye this weekend.
4 At the Natural History Museum we saw an amazing _____.
5 We're having _____ for dinner tonight.

Grammar

5 Circle the correct words.
1. I need (to use) / use the bathroom.
2. Do you want *pancakes* / *eat pancakes* for breakfast?
3. He needs *to* / *a* new mobile phone.
4. What does she need *to buy* / *food* from the market?
5. They want *going* / *to go* to London this summer.
6. My sister needs *wear glasses* / *glasses*. She can't see the board.
7. We need *to clean the car* / *the car to clean*. It's very dirty.
8. He doesn't *want* / *need* to go out tonight. He's tired after the football match.

6 Put the words in the correct order to make sentences.
1. London Eye / want / go on / I / to / the
   I want to go on the London Eye.
2. you / an / Do / mp3 player / need
   _____?
3. want / tonight / She / to / doesn't / film / see / the
   _____.
4. a / They / orange juice / of / want / glass
   _____.
5. He / photos / pay for / to / needs / his
   _____.
6. we / museum / the / Do / visit / need / to
   _____?

7 Answer the questions for you. Use *want* or *need*.
1. What do you want to do this summer?
   Student's own answer.
2. What do you need for your next holiday?
   _____.
3. What does your mum want for her birthday?
   _____.
4. Where do you need to go to buy clothes?
   _____.
5. Where does your family want to go on holiday?
   _____.
6. What do you need to make your favourite food?
   _____.
7. Which city do you want to visit most?
   _____.

8 Complete the email with these words.

> ~~Dear Julie~~   Give   I have to   It was really nice
> Love   Say hello   Thank you   Write

New Reply

¹ *Dear Julie*,

Welcome back to England. ² _____ for your nice postcard. ³ _____ to hear from you and to read about your holiday in France. The castle you visited is very beautiful.

I'm on holiday in Glasgow. It's the largest city in Scotland. There are lots of things to do here. There's a big park called Kelvingrove. It's fantastic. Yesterday, we went for a boat trip on the River Clyde. That was exciting!

⁴ _____ go now because we're going to the Science Museum in half an hour.
⁵ _____ to all your family and
⁶ _____ my love to your brother.
⁷ _____ to me soon.
⁸ _____,
Sara

93

Review 10

Vocabulary

1 Complete the paragraph with holiday words.

Dear Pat,
How are you? I'm very excited. I'm going to a ¹ c a m p s i t e in France with my family tomorrow.
It's near a beach with pretty ²s _ _ _ _ _ _ on the ³s _ _ _ _. I'm going to go swimming every day, so I need my ⁴s _ _ _ _ _ _ _ _ _. I must wear a ⁵c _ _ _ and sit under an ⁶u _ _ _ _ _ _ _ _ _ when it's very hot. I'm going to sleep in a big ⁷t _ _ _ _ in my new red ⁸s _ _ _ _ _ _ _ _ b _ _ _. There are lots of activities at the campsite. I really want to go ⁹h _ _ _ _ _ r _ _ _ _ _ _!
Our clothes are in our ¹⁰s _ _ _ _ _ _ _ _ _ _. We've got our ¹¹ p _ _ _ _ _ _ _ _ _ _ and our plane ¹²t _ _ _ _ _ _ _. We're ready to go! I'll send you a ¹³p _ _ _ _ _ _ _ _ _!
Lots of love,
Daniel

2 Write the words. You can use some words more than once.

| bus ~~coach~~ ferry helicopter ~~lorry~~ |
| motorbike plane ship train |

Which one(s) …
1 have got four wheels?   *coach, lorry*
2 can carry more than ten people?   _____, _____, _____, _____, _____, _____
3 fly in the sky?   _____, _____
4 is the smallest?   _____
5 travel on water?   _____, _____
6 do you need a ticket for?   _____, _____, _____, _____, _____
7 is the fastest?   _____

3 Label the pictures.

1 *fish and chips*   2 _____   3 _____

4 _____   5 _____

Grammar

4 Tick (✓) the sentences about the future.

1 My family and I are visiting Spain next week. ✓
2 I'm lying on the beach. ☐
3 He's not going to school tomorrow. ☐
4 Amy's watching something on TV. ☐
5 We are going to Mars in 2015! ☐
6 The girls are travelling to the concert at the moment. ☐
7 I'm not going to the cinema tonight. ☐
8 Shh! The students are doing a test. ☐

5 Circle the correct words.
1 You *has* / *have* to have a passport to travel to another country.
2 Sandra *doesn't* / *don't* have to cook dinner tonight.
3 My brother has to *studies* / *study* hard for his exams.
4 Do you *have to* / *has to* go to school now?
5 I *doesn't have to* / *don't have to* get up early tomorrow.
6 Does Sue *has to* / *have to* do her homework tonight?
7 My sister and I don't have to *cleaning* / *clean* our room.
8 The boys *have* / *have to* help in the garden.

6 Complete the sentences with *want*, *want to*, *need* or *need to*.
1 I want to go to the beach today.
2 We _____ some eggs to make a cake.
3 They _____ a sandwich for lunch.
4 Do I _____ get a ticket for this bus?
5 Jenny, do you _____ go to the museum with me?
6 Does Joe _____ help with his homework?

7 Choose the correct answers.
1 We're _____ to Italy next week on holiday.
   a fly
   b flying
2 I _____ talk to you about something.
   a need
   b want to
3 Do I _____ go to bed so early, Mum?
   a have to
   b need
4 I _____ your help, Jan.
   a want to
   b need
5 _____ the students studying in the library?
   a Are
   b Will
6 Sally _____ eggs for breakfast.
   a doesn't want
   b doesn't want to

8 Complete the blog.

My Cosmic Blog!

Tell us where you want to go on holiday and why. What will you do there?

For my holiday this year, I want to go to _____. I want to go there because _____.

Also, _____.

When I am there, I _____.

Also, _____.

Colour the Stars

0-8 mistakes:
Brilliant work!

9-15 mistakes:
Great work!

More than 15 mistakes:
Good try. Revise and try again!